Summit Success

Training for Hiking, Mountaineering and Peak Bagging

16 WEEKS TO THE TOP OF THE PEAKS!

©2013-2014 by Charles Miske

ISBN-13: 978-1501039973

ISBN-10: 1501039970

Table of Contents

Table of Contents .... a
Preface i
My Story iii
Disclaimer vii
    Again, in a nutshell viii
Introduction 1
Physical Assessment 3
Training Facilities Assessment 5
Time Assessment 7
Psychological Assessment 10
Hiking Gear Assessment 13
General Principles and Glossary of Training 15
Stretching 20
Training to Hike 21
Establish your own training capacity and level 23
Fat Loss 26
Cardio Tools 28
    Machines to avoid for your base cardio training 31
    Online Cardio Tools 32
Strength Training Tools 33
    Home Style Strength Training Equipment 34
    Gym Style Strength Training Equipment 35
Journaling 37

- Strength Training Journaling Examples ... 37
- Cardio Training Journaling Examples ... 38
  - Example from a Treadmill Workout ... 39
    - Incline Treadmill Calculator Display ... 39
  - Example from a Stairmaster Stepmill Workout ... 40
    - Stepmill Calculator Display ... 40

Light Stretching for Cardio and Strength Training ... 42
- Knee Up, Heel Back ... 43
- Leg Swing ... 44
- Sideways Leg Swing ... 45
- Forward Leaning Glute Swing ... 46
- Sitting Toe Circles ... 47
- Deep Squat Static Stretch ... 48
- Butterfly Static Stretch ... 49
- Hamstring Static Stretch ... 50
- Calf Static Stretch ... 51
- Arm Circles ... 52
- Windmills Front and Rear ... 53
- Ceiling to Floor Presses Palms In and Palms Out ... 54
- Ceiling Press Lean and Floor Press Twist ... 55
- Neck Turn and Neck Tilt ... 56

The Dynamic and Static Stretches Outdoors ... 57
- Knee Up, Heel Back ... 58
- Leg Swing ... 59
- Sideways Leg Swing ... 60

- Forward Leaning Glute Kick 61
- Standing Toe Circles 62
- Deep Squat and Butterfly Static Stretches 63
- Hamstring Static Stretch 64
- Calf Static Stretch 65
- Arm Circles 66
- Windmills Front and Rear 67
- Ceiling to Floor Press 68
- Ceiling Press Lean 69
- Floor Press Twist 70
- Neck Turn 71
- Neck Tilt 72

Cardio Training for the First Four Weeks 73

If you're using a treadmill with a variable incline setting 74
- Treadmill Basic Instructions 75
- Treadmill Math Example 75
- Treadmill Week One 76
- Treadmill Week Two 77
- Treadmill Week Three 77
- Treadmill Week Four 78
- Adjustment Cycle Treadmill Goal Chart 79
- Notes on the Treadmill Program 80

If you're using a Stepmill 81
- Stepmill Training Basic Instructions 81
- Stepmill Math Example 82

- Stepmill Week One 83
  - Stepmill Adjustment Cycle Week One Training Chart 83
- Stepmill Week Two 84
  - Stepmill Adjustment Cycle Week Two Training Chart 84
- Stepmill Week Three 85
  - Stepmill Adjustment Cycle Week Three Training Chart 86
- Stepmill Week Four 87
  - Stepmill Adjustment Cycle Week Four Training Chart 88
- Notes on the Stepmill Program 89

If you're using a Box or Stairs 90

- Stairs Math Example 98
- Box Stepping Math Example 99
- Stairs Week One 100
- Stairs Week Two 100
- Stairs Week Three 101
- Stairs Week Four 101
- Adjustment Cycle Stairs Goal Chart 102
- Box Week One 103
  - Box Adjustment Cycle Week One Training Chart 104
- Box Week Two 105
  - Box Adjustment Cycle Week Two Training Chart 106
- Box Week Three 107
  - Box Adjustment Cycle Week Three Training Chart 108
- Box Week Four 109
  - Box Adjustment Cycle Week Four Training Chart 109

- Box and Stairs Considerations Examined 110
- If you are Running or Walking Outside 111
- 4 Week Adjustment Cycle Calendar 112

Strength Training for the First Four Weeks 113
- Adjustment Cycle Strength Training Considerations 115

Strength Training 116
- Warm-Up 117
  - Elliptical 117
  - Rowing Machine 117
  - Jacob's Ladder 118
  - Walking Lunges 118
  - Box Stepping 118
  - When to Use a Treadmill or Stepmill? 119
- Core Training 119
  - Plank and Side Plank 120
  - Reverse Plank and Superman Plank 122
- Strength Training Exercises 124
  - Romanian Deadlift 124
  - Squat 127
  - Pull-down or Chin-up 130
  - Row 134
  - Chest 137
  - Shoulders 140
  - Calf Raise 145
  - Biceps & Triceps 148

Strength Training Outside with Bands 157

Plank & Side Plank 158

Reverse Plank & Superman Plank 160

Romanian Deadlift 162

Squat 164

Pull-Down 166

Row 168

Chest 170

Shoulders 172

Calf Raise 177

Biceps 181

Triceps 183

Strength Training Outside Wrapping Up 185

General Hiking and Mountaineering Info 186

Leave No Trace Principles 188

The Leave No Trace Seven Principles 190

The Backpack 192

Gear for Hiking and Mountaineering for the Beginner 196

Shoes, Boots and Socks 197

Clothing 201

Snacks and Water 206

Miscellaneous Gear 209

The Twelve Week Program Overview: 216

Chart 1: Vertical Goals using a Treadmill 218

Chart 2: Vertical Goals for Incline Treadmill 220

- Chart 3: Vertical Goals using a Stairmaster Stepmill 221
- Chart 4: Vertical Goals for Box Stepping and Stairs 223
- Other Cardio Machines: 226
- The Remainder of the Sixteen Weeks 227
  - How to use the charts to follow: 227
    - 16% - 4x per Week - no Mileage Deduction for Strength Training 228
    - 16% - 3x per Week - Mileage Deduction for Strength Training 229
    - 4x per Week - no Mileage Deduction for Strength Training 230
    - 9" - 3x per Week - Mileage Deduction for Strength Training 231
  - Treadmill Training for Remaining Twelve Weeks 232
    - 4x per Week - no Mileage Deduction for Strength Training 233
      - Weeks 5-8 233
      - Weeks 9-12 233
      - Weeks 13-16 234
    - 3x per Week - no Mileage Deduction for Strength Training 235
      - Weeks 5-8 235
      - Weeks 9-12 235
      - Weeks 13-16 236
    - 4x per Week - Mileage Deduction for Strength Training 237
      - Weeks 5-8 237
      - Weeks 9-12 237
      - Weeks 13-16 238
    - 3x per Week - Mileage Deduction for Strength Training 239
      - Weeks 5-8 239
      - Weeks 9-12 239

- Weeks 13-16 240
- Incline Treadmill Training for Remaining Twelve Weeks 241
  - 16% - 4x per Week - no Mileage Deduction for Strength Training 242
    - Weeks 5-8 242
    - Weeks 9-12 242
    - Weeks 13-16 243
  - 16% - 3x per Week - no Mileage Deduction for Strength Training 244
    - Weeks 5-8 244
    - Weeks 9-12 244
    - Weeks 13-16 245
  - 16% - 4x per Week - Mileage Deduction for Strength Training 246
    - Weeks 5-8 246
    - Weeks 9-12 246
    - Weeks 13-16 247
  - 16% - 3x per Week - Mileage Deduction for Strength Training 248
    - Weeks 5-8 248
    - Weeks 9-12 248
    - Weeks 13-16 249
  - 20% - 4x per Week - no Mileage Deduction for Strength Training 250
    - Weeks 5-8 250
    - Weeks 9-12 250
    - Weeks 13-16 251
  - 20% - 3x per Week - no Mileage Deduction for Strength Training 252
    - Weeks 5-8 252
    - Weeks 9-12 252

- Weeks 13-16 253

20% - 4x per Week - Mileage Deduction for Strength Training 254
- Weeks 5-8 254
- Weeks 9-12 254
- Weeks 13-16 255

20% - 3x per Week - Mileage Deduction for Strength Training 256
- Weeks 5-8 256
- Weeks 9-12 256
- Weeks 13-16 257

24% - 4x per Week - no Mileage Deduction for Strength Training 258
- Weeks 5-8 258
- Weeks 9-12 258
- Weeks 13-16 259

24% - 3x per Week - no Mileage Deduction for Strength Training 260
- Weeks 5-8 260
- Weeks 9-12 260
- Weeks 13-16 261

24% - 4x per Week - Mileage Deduction for Strength Training 262
- Weeks 5-8 262
- Weeks 9-12 262
- Weeks 13-16 263

24% - 3x per Week - Mileage Deduction for Strength Training 264
- Weeks 5-8 264
- Weeks 9-12 264
- Weeks 13-16 265

Stepmill Training for Remaining Twelve Weeks 266

4x per Week - no Mileage Deduction for Strength Training 267
- Weeks 5-8 267
- Weeks 9-12 267
- Weeks 13-16 268

3x per Week - no Mileage Deduction for Strength Training 269
- Weeks 5-8 269
- Weeks 9-12 269
- Weeks 13-16 270

4x per Week - Mileage Deduction for Strength Training 271
- Weeks 5-8 271
- Weeks 9-12 271
- Weeks 13-16 272

3x per Week - Mileage Deduction for Strength Training 273
- Weeks 5-8 273
- Weeks 9-12 273
- Weeks 13-16 274

Stairs Training for Remaining Twelve Weeks 276

7" - 4x per Week - no Mileage Deduction for Strength Training 277
- Weeks 5-8 277
- Weeks 9-12 277
- Weeks 13-16 278

7" - 3x per Week - no Mileage Deduction for Strength Training 279
- Weeks 5-8 279
- Weeks 9-12 279

Weeks 13-16	280
7" - 4x per Week - Mileage Deduction for Strength Training	**281**
Weeks 5-8	281
Weeks 9-12	281
Weeks 13-16	282
7" - 3x per Week - Mileage Deduction for Strength Training	**283**
Weeks 5-8	283
Weeks 9-12	283
Weeks 13-16	284
9" - 4x per Week - no Mileage Deduction for Strength Training	**285**
Weeks 5-8	285
Weeks 9-12	285
Weeks 13-16	286
9" - 3x per Week - no Mileage Deduction for Strength Training	**287**
Weeks 5-8	287
Weeks 9-12	287
Weeks 13-16	288
9" - 4x per Week - Mileage Deduction for Strength Training	**289**
Weeks 5-8	289
Weeks 9-12	289
Weeks 13-16	290
9" - 3x per Week - Mileage Deduction for Strength Training	**291**
Weeks 5-8	291
Weeks 9-12	291
Weeks 13-16	292

Box Stepping Training for Remaining 12 Weeks 293

12" - 4x per Week - no Mileage Deduction for Strength Training 294

- Weeks 5-8 294
- Weeks 9-12 294
- Weeks 13-16 295

12" - 3x per Week - no Mileage Deduction for Strength Training 296

- Weeks 5-8 296
- Weeks 9-12 296
- Weeks 13-16 297

12" - 4x per Week - Mileage Deduction for Strength Training 298

- Weeks 5-8 298
- Weeks 9-12 298
- Weeks 13-16 299

12" - 3x per Week - Mileage Deduction for Strength Training 300

- Weeks 5-8 300
- Weeks 9-12 300
- Weeks 13-16 301

15" - 4x per Week - no Mileage Deduction for Strength Training 302

- Weeks 5-8 302
- Weeks 9-12 302
- Weeks 13-16 303

15" - 3x per Week - no Mileage Deduction for Strength Training 304

- Weeks 5-8 304
- Weeks 9-12 304
- Weeks 13-16 305

- 15" - 4x per Week - Mileage Deduction for Strength Training ... 306
  - Weeks 5-8 ... 306
  - Weeks 9-12 ... 306
  - Weeks 13-16 ... 307
- 15" - 3x per Week - Mileage Deduction for Strength Training ... 308
  - Weeks 5-8 ... 308
  - Weeks 9-12 ... 308
  - Weeks 13-16 ... 309

Ending the Sixteen Weeks ... 310

Mixing it up ... 311

Now What? ... 312

About the Author ... 313

Training for Hiking, Mountaineering, and Peak Bagging – by Charles Miske

Preface

I began this project in 2012 after having discussed the fitness aspects of learning to hike and climb while losing 60 pounds and achieving many of the dreams I'd had in my youth. In 2013 I compiled a PDF that I sent to several of my friends, and opened up for free download on my website, currently found at http://sevensummitsbody.com/summitsuccess. After about 200 downloads I closed the page and waited for comments to roll in. I was not disappointed at all.

After a summer of taking notes on the people who were out there actually doing it and making some good progress, I began rewriting this book. Since a few of the people I was writing for were doing their first Colorado Fourteener, I aimed the next version directly at them as:

COUCH TO COLORADO FOURTEENER TRAINING PROGRAM

That was great and it actually gave me the direction for the book. If you notice that a lot of the text is about climbing a Fourteener, then keep in mind that's who it was originally written for. I have gone through it and changed up a few things that were too specifically about Fourteeners, but please keep an open mind if you begin to feel like I'm forcing the Fourteeners down your throat.

As soon as I opened up the beta program for a select group of paid subscribers it became obvious that I needed to adjust the focus away from the Colorado Fourteeners and onto training for any mountain adventure and it became:

MOUNTAINEERING FITNESS: BEGINNER TRAINING MANUAL

This was pretty awesome for a lot of the human guinea pigs working on the program. I got a few minor complaints about it though, so I posted a survey and got a slew of responses pointing out that the word "mountaineering" seemed too serious and scared a lot of beginners away. From that series of exchanges the current title evolved, blending the best suggestions into what I now feel is the best title for this work:

SUMMIT SUCCESS: TRAINING FOR HIKING, MOUNTAINEERING AND PEAK BAGGING

That might be a bit long, and Amazon and Createspace might have a few little issues but we can overcome that, right?

I thought I'd share this with you in case you have been following along on my Facebook Page at http://facebook.com/SevenSummitsBody and became confused at all the titles I've been discussing with all of you. Otherwise, please go LIKE it and get involved in the discussions. We'd love to have you on board.

I hope this book is all that I have promised, and that you get the best training available in a book of its type. The primary focus is on the concept of Vertical Training versus Horizontal Training. I feel that the best success in the mountains and on the trails is through a mixture of the two.

When I was training for Elbrus Race 2010 I was doing a lot of Vertical Training but not a lot of Horizontal Training. I was pretty quick on the uphill portions of the trail but didn't have the endurance necessary to do the whole round trip ascent plus descent in as good a style as I wished. This was especially obvious on Elbrus in 2012 when I did way too much acclimatization hiking and wore myself out before I even got onto the mountain.

This training plan is the result of my own experiments on my own body. Please read it, and try to follow it as best you can. I'm a numbers kind of guy so it might seem a bit heavy on the 5th Grade math, but I explain it all in a fairly simple manner that most of my guinea pigs have been comfortable with. The best thing about it is that with a little bit of your own ingenuity you can fudge the math a bit and turn it into a 20 week or 12 week program. You can use my math to create the program that will work best for you.

I wish you the best success in using it. I have thought of that with every page I wrote. Thanks.

Charles Miske

My Story

Late in the summer of 2005 I weighed 220 pounds, mostly gained from working 60 hour weeks at a tech job. I attempted Castle Peak, a Colorado Fourteener with a road up to 12,000' good for 4x4 vehicles. I didn't summit, because I was really out of shape. I started out too quickly, since in my own mind I was still young and strong and fast. I got lost, lacked confidence on the rough trail near the top, and ran out of time. I didn't have a headlamp with to negotiate the trail in the dark. I was completely unprepared.

A few weeks later I did manage to hike to the summit of Torreys, another Colorado Fourteener. I camped near the trailhead, got a very early start, and allowed more time to go up. Sadly, it took nearly twice as long to descend to the trailhead as it took to get to the top. Going down was really hard on my body, which was quite beat up by the time I got back to the car.

This sorry state of physical conditioning was frustrating to me, because just five years before I had climbed four of the 14ers in one summer, and was among the faster hikers on the trail. I guess that's what happens when you abandon your fitness in return for success at a desk job. A long time ago I had a personal trainer certification. I had exercised off and on since I was 19. I had been a year-round bicycle commuter. I had run several 5K and 8K races and done well. I never even noticed that I had gained so much fat and become so unfit.

The next fall, 2006, after ballooning up to nearly 240 pounds, my daughter was born. When I looked at her little face, I realized that I had put my health at risk, and if I wanted to watch her grow up, I would need to make some serious changes, starting right that minute. I finally had the motivation to begin a fitness program designed to get me to the top of the mountain. With my love of hiking and climbing, I knew that if I were to focus on the rewards of trips to the mountains, I could sustain a program to return to the "me" I used to be. Over the next four years I lost 60 pounds, and kept it off for another four years as of this writing in summer 2014. That being said, I can't imagine gaining any of it back.

During my fat loss journey I started took up several sports and adventure activities. I've climbed rock and ice, on glaciers and couloirs. I've run on the road in 10K and half marathons. I've run on trails in 10K, half marathon and full marathon races. I successfully ran the Qualifier for Elbrus Race 2010, and finished in 5th place for Elbrus Race 2013. I trained the 3rd place finisher for that race, one of my proudest achievements in training an elite athlete.

I studied a lot of different theories from articles by trainers, coaches and teachers. I experimented with several different training and eating theories. I have long since figured out how I could have sped up my progress quite a bit, and I know that in general you too can have the same results that I got, only in less time and with less wasted effort. In this book I will focus more on the training aspects of the program. If you want more information about how to lose fat quickly using proven, sound science please check out my other book, a food portion control program for fast, efficient, fat loss.

The 100 Calorie Diet Plan

We began discussing this journey with a Colorado Fourteener. Let's start on the path to achieve that goal now, and if climbing a 14er is the carrot on your stick, then by all means, let's get you to the top.

Photo, next page, me at 235 pounds at the beginning of my mountaineering training adventure.

Summit Success

Training for Hiking, Mountaineering, and Peak Bagging – by Charles Miske

Disclaimer

Once upon a time I was a Certified Personal Trainer. Back then, around the turn of the century, I had been working as a Tech Support Manager at a software company. It downsized and outsourced just about everything but the sales staff. I had a little income teaching Kung Fu in my garage and had developed some private web design and programming clients so I didn't really need a lot more money. One of my family members wanted to become a personal trainer so I studied along with them, took the test with them, and next thing you know I was certified.

I let the certification expire though when I was hired by an out of state startup to run a division of their company. It was obvious that I would make a lot more money as their Tech Support Manager. I still read and studied a lot though in personal training issues. I even took a few Kung Fu students in my new home and used some of my hard-earned personal training theory on them. That lasted until I got involved as a partner in another startup and ended up in the classic IPO mode of 80 hour weeks trying to figure out how to make it all pay off.

I also didn't go to medical school or get a degree in any health related field. The information presented in this book is a compilation of the knowledge I gained from several different seminars and workshops I attended over the years as I studied to get my personal trainer certification, from seminars I attended as someone interested in the extremes of physical and athletic performance, as someone who had the inkling of an idea that I'd be writing this and other training plans, and from practical hands-on experience with both myself, and the athletes I consult and coach for.

Due to, or in spite of, all of that I can't promise anything, or make any claims of a medical or professional nature. Your results are completely up to you. I also can't promise that you will not be injured in any way or capacity, mental or physical. I suggest that you get clearance to accept the challenge of this program from a properly licensed medical professional before you begin. If you need assistance from an Adaptive Training Specialist, please have them contact me for suggestions and advice on how to accommodate any special needs you might have.

Having assumed that you are cleared by a qualified medical professional I hope that you agree that I cannot reasonably be held accountable for what you do with the information presented here, which is basically a collection of traditional workout and training methods presented in a program format that I personally feel for myself is suitably applicable to climbing one or more of the Colorado Fourteeners, or a similar goal of a long day hike with quite a bit of vertical ascent and descent.

As the car commercials so carefully state in the fine print "Your Mileage May Vary" (YMMV). Be aware, alert, and careful not to hurt yourself in any way. I would feel bad, if nothing else.

Again, in a nutshell

- no promises
- no guarantees
- get permission
- don't hurt yourself

I trust that you will use common sense and be aware of danger to prevent injury to yourself or others. I trust that you will check out anything you are unsure of with a qualified professional, either medical or fitness. Since I won't be there to keep an eye on you you'll have to be self-aware enough to do that for me. I also can't accommodate every special need in this book of a general nature. I am however interested in your own unique story, so please, take a minute to drop by the Facebook Page or the Website and share it all of us, or just me if that's more comfortable to you.

Introduction

Do you want to climb a mountain? Have you climbed one before? Maybe when you were younger or quite a bit more fit? What about a long hike like the Wonderland Trail, nearly 100 miles circumnavigating Mount Rainier with 22,000' of elevation gain. Then there are the classics like The Pacific Crest Trail, the Appalachian Trail, and the Colorado Trail. Each of these is a worthy goal and if you dream of someday accomplishing one of these then I hope to be able to help you begin here.

And by begin, I'm assuming you're not all that ready to climb or hike one of these right now, since you're reading this. I could be wrong though since quite a few of my beta program participants are trail runners and mountaineers looking for a different perspective on training. In either case I'm here to help you become fit enough to climb a good size mountain or take a long hike.

This program is 16 weeks long. You can start it any time. I hope you never really ever quit this program so I've provided instructions on how to taper back to a maintenance variation on the program so that you can live a normal life while staying fit enough that you can drop right back into it and peak in time for your attempt at a large hike or climb.

I hope I provide enough information for you to continue to grow in fitness and health. If you need to grow new muscle, I can help you. If you need to shred off some fat, I can help with that too. Even if you need to do both I can get you where you want to go. But let's get back to that trail now.

"The Mountains are calling and I must go." -- John Muir

If you're wanting to do a hike on a bigger type mountain, something to prove to yourself that you have what it takes, I recommend climbing a Colorado Fourteener. Otherwise spelled 14'er or 14er according to Google. This is a peak with a summit over 14,000' above sea level. Officially and unofficially, there are different rules to determine if it's a "summit" or just a bump on the ridge of another big mountain. There are over 50 such mountains in Colorado. The exact number depends on which list you accept. That number is really only important if you're going to try to do all of them. If you just want to have a great day out in the mountains with the potential for a beautiful view, maybe see some mountain goats or pika, and a great physical challenge, there are lots of mountains to choose from. Many of them have decent road access and a trail that most people of at least average fitness can successfully hike in a single day.

I noticed that there are several "Couch to…" books and guides and manuals out there. You could go to a running website and order "Couch to 5K", "Couch to 10K", "Couch to Half Marathon", "Couch to Marathon" etc. In my mind climbing a Fourteener is roughly equivalent to running in a half marathon. Yes, thousands of people do it each week, but to someone who has never run one before, it seems rather extreme. In general a good training program during a period of 12-16 weeks could get you from the couch to finishing one. Maybe not in a great time, but finishing a half marathon is possible with about 4 months of training. Climbing a Colorado 14er with 4 months of training is realistic. I suppose that just about any similar mountain climbing goal would be quite possible in that time frame.

If you want to get off the couch and onto the top of one of the highest mountains in the Continental USA, let me help you get in shape over the next 16 weeks. Make a commitment to get on the program, and at the end test yourself. Test your fitness and endurance by hiking one of the Colorado Fourteeners

If you're looking for another big mountain that is requires no special skills other than walking on unstable terrain, there are a few 14'ers in California too. There are mountains with decent trails and about 3000' of elevation gain in several other parts of the USA.

If you're looking for a hiking challenge I heartily recommend a section of the Colorado Trail. In some sections you can do relatively simple day hikes that are well worth the effort with beautiful views. Similarly a section of the Wonderland Trail, while crowded most of the season, is an amazing accomplishment for a day hike.

One thing I need to emphasize here is that this book is focused more on day hiking than on overnight trips. For one thing I'm creating a training manual for first-timers. For another it's a completely different set of skills and I will cover that in my next book in the series, oriented more toward multi-day adventures, trekking, backpacking and mountaineering trips.

Now before we begin, one of the first things you want to do is find out exactly where you stand physically right this minute. Or at least this week. Keep in mind that while I have taken workshops on assessing a personal training client, I can't really assess you in person right now, so I'm going to have to trust you to do this for me, okay? It's very important for both of us that you start out on the right foot. I don't want you to try going any faster or farther than your body is able. Please read and heed the next chapter. Do not proceed with the actual training without doing so. Thanks.

Physical Assessment

First of all, what is your current physical or medical condition? Have you had a physical recently? If so did you pass? If not, would you pass a physical? Would a legally licensed medical professional clear you to participate in the training and eventual hike similar to that up a 14er? If the answer is no, then why? Is it something that would prevent you from hiking? From working out? Be honest. If you for sure have or would pass a physical, awesome – I said I would trust you. If the honest answer is that you don't know, go schedule a physical. I'll wait.

Good, you're back – I'm going to assume that means you've been cleared by your qualified medical professional to continue with the program. Consider that there are things a doctor can't know in the office, including your potential response to altitude and how likely you are to get Acute Mountain Sickness – or AMS. Even seasoned, experienced mountaineers can have a bad reaction to altitude now and then, without any apparent reason. I know, because it's happened to me a couple of times. There also is no way to tell how your body will respond to extremes in weather. I've seen really strong hikers pretty much fall completely apart in freezing rain and start shivering uncontrollably until they could get into their car with the heater on. This isn't something you learn in a physician's office. You find out when you're in the thick of it.

Physically, you'll need to be able to carry approximately 15 pounds, hike about 10 miles, ascend and descend 3,000' or so, all in 9 hours or less. This assumes a summer hike on or in the vicinity of a simple Colorado Fourteener. One thing to consider, for speed, is that typically in July and August here in Colorado we have the "Monsoon" weather pattern as it's called locally. Around noon a lightning storm is quite common and you want to be at least down into the trees below 12,000' before that happens. If you plan on a 6:00 AM start, that means you want to be on the summit in less than 5 hours, to allow an hour to get back down into the trees.

There are several complicated and sometimes expensive tests to determine your fitness levels. At this stage of the game I don't think there's that much value in determining something like your Maximum Heart Rate at Lactate Threshold. If you're obsessed with numbers and graphs and stuff, then go for it. For the rest of you though, don't sweat it unless your medical professional insists. We'll talk later about how to figure out your own speeds and weights for training.

For right now though, the most important question is: Are you physically capable of doing the training program as outlined in this book? I'm not going to force you into some massive program of doubling our daily goals. What that means is that if your goal is to ascend 3000' while covering 5 miles of trail we're not going to train by going 6000' over 10 miles. While running. In a 30 lb. backpack. Yeah. We're not going to do that. I'll explain why later.

Training for Hiking, Mountaineering, and Peak Bagging – by Charles Miske

While I've been focusing a great deal of my book on a Colorado 14er, and I've explained why a number of times, I'd also like to point out that our long term goal of hiking 10 miles with an ascent and descent of 4,000' is an excellent physical accomplishment that you could be proud of. You can find popular day hikes in Maine, New Hampshire, Nevada, California, or Montana. Heck, you could find them just about anywhere there are steep hills and dirt trails. Sorry Florida…

Training Facilities Assessment

Next we need to determine what you have to work out with. Based on my experiences losing sixty pounds of fat and keeping it off, the single best thing I could do to increase the speed of my own progression and success was to train at home. If you have no equipment at all, either cardio or weights, this is still an option we can cover in the program phase.

If you already have some equipment that's great. You might have to do some minor adjustments between my program and your equipment. If you do have equipment and have used it, I'll assume here that you have a pretty good idea how it works and how to make it work sometimes in an "other than as intended" way. A way which I probably shouldn't recommend. As I mentioned before, don't get hurt and please don't blame me if you cook up some wild combination of training you found on a YouTube video. You didn't see the ending when the barbells burst into flames and the cat booked it out of the room knocking the camera over.

Remember that YouTube is a wealth of information on different exercise and equipment combinations. Remember too that each trainer has their own methodology and some have sound, valid perspectives, and some are just whacked. You get what you pay for, and YouTube is free. I do fitness consultations with clients as part of my business, so that's also an option if you're totally lost and confused and want or need to make faster progress without a lot of time wasted messing around trying to figure out how to do a Bench Press without a bench, for example.

I also can't show each and every variation of each and every exercise, depending on whether you have kettle bells, or dumbbells, or a selectorized weight stack. At least without turning this into a very boring 900 page book that I can't afford to publish and you can't afford to purchase. I can give you general ideas, and it's up to you to figure out how to make your gear work. Or the gear at the gym. Or at your buddy's house. Or at your mom's house. If you put your mind to it you can make it work.

WHERE THERE'S A WILL THERE'S A WAY. - PROVERB

If you have a gym membership, that's good too. Maybe better than good because you have a few more options to choose from, and if something isn't working you can make changes on the fly and essentially for free. As an example, if the straight bar is giving your elbows heck, you can find some variation of curved bar that might be easier on them.

I will also be giving suggestions in the various training descriptions for different things you can do there. I know from my own experience and talking to quite a few traveling athletes that after training in different gyms all around the country, you eventually get to where you can just go in and figure out all the machines and weights in only a few seconds. There really isn't all that much difference once you get past the colors and shapes. At first though, you might need a little help.

Most gyms offer free or inexpensive orientation tours for members or prospective members. Take advantage of one of these resources, even if you think you know all of the equipment there. You might learn something valuable, making it way worth it in saved time and effort.

I want you to think about all of this now before we begin. I don't really want you to go buy anything, or sign up at a gym, unless you've been looking for an excuse to do so. I also want you to promise to stick with it long after your Fourteener summit or dream hike has passed under your feet. I actually don't want you to ever quit, but for right now focus on the goal and keep in mind that there will be something beyond the goal.

One of my goals as your virtual coach is to get you to an excellent state of base fitness leaning slightly toward walking up and down hills on rough terrain. With that base you can progress to any number of options. The world is at your doorstep. Which way will you go next?

Time Assessment

How much time do you need? How much time do you have? It's almost that simple. This training manual includes a really basic fitness plan and assumes you're pretty much a beginner or low intermediate as far as training goes. At that level you get a lot of bang for the buck as far as your time investment goes. Something along the lines of one half hour to one hour for four to six days a week should do it in the first third to half of the program. As the program progresses to near the end of the 16 weeks you might be training for 2 hours 3 to 4 times a week alternated with 1 hour or less on the other days.

You work your way into it slowly though. The entire 16 week plan gradually increases in intensity and duration. The focus is slightly more on duration than on time though, since you don't need a lot of strength to carry a 12 pound pack and you're going pretty slowly in the big scheme of things. The strength training could even be done at the exact same level over the course of the plan without increasing anything. We're really working our way toward what amounts to an eight hour hike with a fairly light backpack. With that in mind we'll gently work our way up to 2 or so hours 4 times a week.

Seriously though. That's not all that much time in the big scheme of things. Remember, competitive amateur triathletes will train twice that or more every single day. If you're that strapped for time that you are struggling with squeezing in an hour or two every day, I can offer some suggestions for you to consider implementing in your life, starting right from day one of the program.

One thing that can save a lot of time is to multi-task. Try doing other things while you're training. Cardio machines make this a bit easier than if you were outside. If you're used to reading the newspaper, reading it is easy enough on a recumbent stationary bike. Some people can read them on treadmills and Stepmills. Books and magazines can be read on almost any cardio machine that does not absolutely require you to cling to the rails to preserve your life.

Audio books are an excellent choice for any cardio machine or even outdoor training and are among my very favorite ways to get in my weekly reading.

"IF YOU CAN GET YOURSELF TO READ 30 MINUTES A DAY, YOU'RE GOING TO DOUBLE YOUR INCOME EVERY YEAR." -- BRIAN TRACY

If you normally watch some favorite TV shows, set the DVR for your show time and then watch it while training. You can watch them simply enough on any cardio machine except the climbing type like Jacob's Ladder or Treadwall. I've even done this weight training while in my own garage and basement. You can stream or download some shows to a tablet and watch that, even at the gym, resting it on the shelf that many gym cardio machines have for books. Be careful though that they are securely set on that shelf or bracket. You don't want it to fall into your feet or pedals or belt and possibly damage you or the tablet.

If you can trade some time that you usually use for entertainment or education, you can make this work and hardly notice a lot of the time spent on training. Just be careful if you're using a machine that is easy to injure yourself on if you have a lapse in attention. I don't want you to get so excited over a TV show that you fall off the back of a treadmill. I've seen this happen a few times now. Worse in my opinion is falling off the back of a Stepmill. It's a bit steeper and has a little ways further to the floor.

A bit more extreme would be if you were to completely skip TV, or online poker, Pinterest, or other things that you weigh to be less important than your fitness. You'll be amazed at how much time you really do have. I used to watch some TV and have had a few favorite shows over the years. Now I watch almost none at all unless I'm stuck on a treadmill or Stairmaster. That alone has given me several hours a week to focus on the things that really matter to me, like my family. Sometimes family time is hanging out on the sofa together watching AFV. I really don't want you to lose time with your family or work, so please try to arrange to lose the time you would normally consider to be a waste (like TV) first. Do not get divorced or fired over this goal.

"IT IS WELL TO BE UP BEFORE DAYBREAK, FOR SUCH HABITS CONTRIBUTE TO HEALTH, WEALTH, AND WISDOM." -- ARISTOTLE

On my various Facebook pages, I get to read complaints from lots of people about hitting the snooze button 8 times every morning. Wow. What's' up with that? Do they dislike the daily events of their lives so much they want to avoid greeting it every day? Holy snot! If you multiply 8 x 5:00 you end up with 40:00 – that's forty minutes of the day down the drain. You could have just counted your sleep time for recovery and set your alarm for forty minutes later. It would have been more productive than the half-sleep between slapping the snooze button over and over.

Better yet, get up, get moving. There are several amazing health benefits from an early start to the day. It seems like every time I look at personal trainer news there is some new study about the benefits of training early in the day. Some of these studies are controversial of course, and in my own opinion vary widely based on individual traits.

An example of controversial studies are the alleged fat burning benefits of slow versus fast cardio and fasted versus fed training. It would drive you nuts trying to do both simultaneously. Thank goodness we're not talking about fat much in this book though, so let's just skip over that for now.

"EARLY TO BED AND EARLY TO RISE, MAKES A MAN HEALTHY, WEALTHY AND WISE" - BENJAMIN FRANKLIN

A workout in the early morning is the best way to prepare for an energized productive day. Go for a walk and watch the sun rise. See how beautiful it is. Feel the early morning air as the sun changes the texture and smell and sense of it. You will grow to love it. Like I briefly touched on previously, it's commonly stated that triathletes are among the most conscientious time managers and successful in business, family, and training. Triathletes train hard in 3 disciplines, all of which require hours a day of training to achieve the highest levels of the sport. If they can make their lives work while training 4 to 6 hours a day almost every single day, you can squeeze in 1 to 2 hours for 16 weeks.

If I can make it work while squeezing in 4-6 hours a day training for Elbrus Race in 2010 and 2013, then just about anyone can squeeze in an hour or two here and there. I know you can. Trust me on this and we'll get along fine. Speaking of which, next we need to see how mentally strong you are.

Psychological Assessment

This is the toughest, but maybe most important qualification. How prepared are you mentally? How much do you want it? How bad can it get before you quit? Are you motivated to hit the summit with energy to spare? To get down as fast as you got up, or even faster? To hike from trailhead to trailhead and make your deadline for your ride home? Can you suffer just a little bit now to save yourself a great deal of suffering later? Can you enjoy the beautiful view from the summit of a Colorado 14er or any other beautiful tall mountain, saddle, or pass, and say to yourself "It was worth every second" with a huge grin on your face? Can you say that same thing after any 10 mile hike under any conditions? Rain, sleet, wind, snow, hail? I've had them all and more in my world travel adventures.

I can tell you from personal experience that it is worth it. To me there is no doubt. That's where you need to be as well. The handful of people that I've helped to get to the summit know it's true. The trail runners I've consulted with for training support all know it's true. If you can get your mind wrapped around that, you'll probably prove it to yourself too.

A dream doesn't become reality through magic; it takes sweat, determination and hard work.
-- Colin Powell

Recently I attended a workshop run by famous climber Steve House to introduce his new book *"Training for the New Alpinism"* and one of the key takeaways from his presentation was that with any big program you need an adjustment period. Since I had been in a relatively trained condition for much of my adult life, having begun running at 19 and weight training at 21, I had nearly forgotten what it was like to be completely untrained.

Even when I had become a cubicle dweller, and first started working back into fitness when I had my epiphany in 2006, I just started training and slowly worked my way back into it. Friends, family and work just evolved with me. I didn't think too much about it at the time. It just happened and it all worked out.

So considering that not everyone can do that, for my program I have included a 4 week adjustment period. This will be the first 4 weeks of the 16 total. That will leave you 12 weeks after you adjust to training to truly get in shape for your hiking goal.

During this adjustment time you will:
- learn how to train on your available equipment
- learn what weights and settings are appropriate for you

- figure out how to squeeze training into your lifestyle
- help your friends and loved ones accept and support your training

For psychological support, it's very important that your friends and loved ones are there backing you up at every step of the way. My wife encouraged me to go on climbing trips and take climbing classes along my own body transformation path. She helped me get going on the days I felt like I had been hit by a truck. She helped me realize when I needed extra rest days. My kids knew that when I was on the treadmill I needed peace and aloneness. "Me Time" was essential during those days of hard training. The love and support of my family was instrumental in my success. Now, these several (8 as of this writing) years later, I am passing on these support system suggestions to you and hope that you can evolve into the trained and fit individual you see yourself as.

Your support system will be an integral aspect of your transformation. In all fairness though, you need to be up front with everyone you associate with. So that when your friends want to go hang out in bars till 1:00 AM and your training time is 6:00 AM, you can just flat out say you need your sleep. True friends will support you. True loved ones will support you. This is just an example, and I'm sure I don't have to give others to illustrate it more fully to you, do I?

You need your sleep, you need your training time, you need your training clothes and equipment clean and in good condition at the time you need it to be. You need to make sure that no one will interfere with it. You need to make sure that your needs do not interfere with theirs. Make it work. It's worth it.

Being honest up front about it is the best policy. Trust me. The burden is on you. Be a good friend. Be a good spouse. Be a good sibling. Be a good son or daughter. These are the things that will inspire others to follow your example in their own success quests. Climbing a mountain is symbolic of the path to success in every venture. Remember that when you are having an off day.

Psychologically, you also need to accept what this training program is and does, and what it requires from you. A long time ago a friend of a friend came to me for training advice, since I was climbing a lot, and hiking up mountains a lot. A lot in this case was about a mountain every other week and rock climbing every other day. He was planning on climbing a 13,000' peak in a nearby state and asked what he could do right now to get in shape for it.

After assessing his current circumstances and physical condition, I suggested that he put a 25 pound bag of rice into his backpack and walk for an hour along the creek near his house every morning before work. I asked that he also do it again in the evening after work. I told him that after ten weeks of that he'd be in great shape for his peak.

He couldn't accept it though. It was too simple. He couldn't wrap his head around the simplicity of rice in a backpack along the creek. I think that's part of the reason so many people fall for the coolest latest buzzword hyped program. By latching onto the coolest thing they inherit some of the coolness. Coolness possibly won't be enough to get you up the mountain though. Stick to the basics. They've worked for at least a hundred years and more. They'll keep working in spite of the coolness that's on TV or in the "box" today.

That's why this program is so basically simple. I want you to succeed in spite of yourself. I planned around the simplest equipment. I provide the specifics for treadmills, Incline Treadmills, Stepmills, stairs, boxes and hiking in your own hills. If you can follow this simple plan from week to week, for 16 weeks, you will most assuredly be ready for the trail.

Hiking Gear Assessment

Originally I wrote this very specific to climbing a Colorado 14er in the peak summer season. Now that this book has evolved into a full-fledged training for hiking book, I'm going to expand this quite a bit.

In order to climb a Colorado 14er, during the summer, under normal conditions on one of the simpler routes, you will need to carry a bare minimum of gear. For an average day hike in much of the continental USA you'll have to make some minor adjustments, allowing for local weather conditions. For perspective, I'll show two extremes. There are people who run these mountains in running shoes, shorts and t-shirts, with a small running pack with a couple of small water bottles, a couple of goo packets, and a windbreaker, beanie and gloves in their tiny pack. For trails in warmer climates with little probability of rain or snow, they might carry quite a bit less.

On the other extreme you'll see those with heavy leather hiking boots, and 50 liter backpacks stuffed to the brim with stoves and fuel, 6 liters of water, a couple packets of freeze-dried food, a bivy sack, large down jacket, change of clothes, and all of the other 35 pounds of survival gear, just in case. I kid you not. You'll even see this type of hiker in relatively warm and dry canyons in South-Eastern Utah. For a day hike. Yeah.

I myself fall into the first group. A very long time ago I hiked to the bottom of the Grand Canyon and out again with a couple nights over the Rim. I think my backpack weighed close to 60 pounds. That was a long time ago. In Alaska on Denali I had about 80 pounds in my backpack and another 40 on the sled at the beginning of the trip. There though you'll have to carry every single thing you need to survive in brutal conditions for three weeks.

Now, in the interest of safe and comfortable hiking, for most normal people, under most normal conditions, I think that at a reasonable minimum, you should have:

- waterproof windbreaker
- thin down or synthetic jacket
- hat/gloves/face mask
- extra socks
- 3 liters of water
- 9 snack items about 200 calories each
- headlamp/flashlight

The above and a few other extras should be less than 12 pounds in a 16 liter or so pack. These are geared slightly toward high country Rocky Mountain hiking. In the PNW you might want a heavier rain jacket. In Maine you might want a bug proof face net. You need to take the responsibility to find out for yourself what works best in your area, or the area you plan to hike in.

For steep terrain I recommend trekking poles, preferably two, but one will do. They are great for a bit of extra stability, and if you're on the older and creakier side, they take the load off your knees on the descent which can be a blessing to some of us.

I hate having to make a boot recommendation. I really do. I myself have discovered that in general I do best in running shoes. I actually own no boots that fit in between running shoes and ice climbing boots. Even my ice climbing boots have very soft ankles with only stiff hard shells around the heel and toe to clamp the crampons onto. I have been over 16,000' up to 18,500' in running shoes several times, even with aluminum crampons on. I am a strong advocate of strong feet and ankles and the lightest shoe you can get by on.

You of course will have to decide for yourself how strong your ankles and feet are, and how much protection and support you will need. Some of the trails are rocky with loose gravel and dirt. That being said, I've seen people doing Fourteeners in sandals and skateboard shoes. I do recommend that whatever you are going to be hiking in should also become your training footwear. Some shoes need breaking in and others don't so you'll have to make that decision too. I'd hate for you to start a long hike in brand new shoes and discover they don't work when you're at your furthest point from the car. Find out while training near home.

For the rest of your gear, you shouldn't have to buy anything special, but again, some people totally respond to reward systems, and later we'll discuss some more of my ideas of what's important in the way of gear. A reward system is when you buy yourself toys (gear) when you stick to your goals for a set period of time or accomplishment.

I do recommend though that you train your cardio in your backpack after the initial 4 week cycle, and that if you can walk outside for training, you use your trekking poles. Using your trekking poles inside your own garage or basement might work for some people, but you definitely would get a talking to if you try using them in a commercial facility, even with rubber bumpers on the ends.

So if you get nothing else now, you will need those two items before the others. I include instructions in the training plan section on when to start using the backpack and you can figure out the poles on your own.

Otherwise, let this small chapter be a teaser to get your mind working while we begin the training program. If you are one of those who respond to rewards, print out some online catalog photos of your dream gear and stick those up next to a sticky note outlining the small goal associated with it. Then buy it when you've reached that milestone in your training. Rewards can be good. Use them if needed.

General Principles and Glossary of Training

Let's get something straight up front. Define what we're doing here. These are my definitions and might be a bit different from those of a TV Guru or other fitness professional. Please don't get hung up over it. Think of it as a translation page. Check here if something in the book doesn't make as much sense as you'd like.

Exercising is movement that takes effort or work over time. Riding your bike, walking, gardening – all can be forms of exercise. If you're unconvinced, just ask someone wearing one of those all-day calorie counting wristbands. They can increase their stats by spinning their office chair for a half hour.

Working Out is methodical exercise done under controlled circumstances. Going to the gym every day and riding a treadmill and a few weight machines would be working out. Walking around the block every morning to buy a newspaper is working out.

Program is a workout plan extended over time. A 12 week "Up Your Bench Press" plan is a Program. A proper program would include rest and up and down cyclical variations in training volume. In other words, a program includes lighter weights every few weeks, since your growth is dependent on resting as much as hard work. Going all-out every workout all the time no matter what is not a program.

Cycle is a period of time that you use a specific program for. One Personal Trainer Truism is that just about anything will work for 3-6 weeks. With that in mind I like to break programs up into 4 or 6 week cycles.

Training is working out with a set athletic goal. Climbing a Colorado Fourteener is an athletic goal. Following a program to get you to that goal is training. So from now on, you're "in training" – not just exercising, not just working out. Keep that mindset – it will help you get through, and it's cool to say when anyone asks what you're doing.

Believe it or not, the average person who is doing "exercise" or "working out" will most likely think hiking to the top of a 14,000' mountain is pretty cool and maybe even extreme.

A few of the key points of training were brought out in the above definitions, but we'll go over them again along with some other important considerations for this training program.

Overload is when you lift more than you are used to. That's usually used in a context about as vague as it sounds. If you were to lift your arms overhead with empty hands, that's "normal" but if you had 10 lb. weights in your hands that would be overload. If you lay down on the floor and then stand up, that's "normal" but if you were to hold a 25 pound sack of rice while doing it that would be overload. Hope that makes sense.

Progressive resistance is when you increase the amount of overload over time. The idea is that your body compensates for the increased load with increased strength and endurance. Sometimes it can also respond with bigger muscles.

Rep is one complete motion in an exercise. In a chin-up, grabbing the bar, raising your chin to the bar, and lowering your feet to the floor would be one rep.

Set is a group of reps followed by rest. In many, if not most, protocols there is no rest between reps in any one set.

RM is the abbreviation for "Reps Max" and is used in combination with a number like this "1RM" which means the amount of weight that you can do one rep, and one rep only, for a given exercise. If you attempted to do 2 you would fail. "10RM" means that you can do 10 reps, and 10 reps only, of a certain weight in a given exercise. If you were to attempt to do 11 you would fail. Someone might have a Deadlift 1RM of 325 pounds, and a 10RM weight of 195 pounds. For the most part I'm including this as a concept, especially if you try to get your exercise information from YouTube or another source. For most beginning trainers it's not so significant and it's difficult at times to determine that number anyway.

VAM is an oddball measurement. It's the Vertical Ascent Meters per hour measurement. 1000 meters in one hour is 1000 VAM. 300 meters in one hour is 300 VAM. If you look at our Fourteener Target we're going to try to go about 3,000' in 4 to 5 hours. We'll round that up to 1000 meters (3281') and divide it by the 4 hours to equal an optimum average pace of 250 VAM. How do you use that? I've created my programs based around achieving that goal. I wrote some simple calculators for the Stepmill and Incline Treadmill to help you convert your workout stats to VAM. You can check your progress by using one of these calculators I posted on the blogs I linked here for you.

Protocol is the basis of the program. It's the combination of weights, sets and reps you use. It's the amount of increased overload you use. It might include the number of seconds you do each section in an exercise movement. Generally there are certain proven protocols you would use for different goals. Bodybuilders, power lifters, endurance athletes, and strongman competitors would all use different protocols much of the time.

General Physical Preparation (GPP) is usually a protocol during which you work a balanced combination of sets and reps to prepare your body for other styles of training. In most training programs it would be the first cycle.

Strength is the amount of weight, or overload, you can move.

Volume is the amount of weight you move over time and distance. If you assume the distance to be the same between workouts and disregard time, the difference in volume between 10 chin-ups and 11 chin-ups is 10%. The difference between doing a set of 5 deadlifts at 100 pounds and a set of 5 deadlifts at 105 pounds is 5%. Time is harder to calculate, but has an effect on some protocols. Doing deadlifts with 30 seconds of rest between sets has a metabolic effect (burns fat) and doing deadlifts with 5 minutes of rest between sets has an anabolic effect (builds muscle). One difference between the two is that with only 30 seconds of rest you aren't able to lift as much weight on a per-rep basis over the given time. Anyway, this is just an introduction to a concept; don't get all hung up over it.

Specificity is how closely related your training is to your athletic goal. If your goal is to run a marathon, running is overall the best training. If your goal is to place in a power lifting championship, then lifting heavy weights is the best training. If your sport of choice is jumping on boxes, then box jumping is the best training. Bicep curls, the exercise of choice in gyms around the nation, have almost nothing to do with running or box jumping.

Accessory training is when you do an exercise that helps a supporting muscle for your chosen athletic endeavor or training goals. If your sport of choice is ice climbing, then pull-ups are a great exercise with a lot of specificity. Since one of the moving parts in a pull-up is the biceps, biceps curls would be part of an accessory training program for climbing. The word accessory implies that this is extra training. You should not turn this into or add it into your main training. A few sets of light biceps curls at the end of a pull-up workout is adequate, but there's no reason in a typical athletic program to take your biceps curls to failure.

Antagonist training is when you train the muscle opposite of the one you train for accessory training. In the example above of training biceps, you could do triceps presses as your antagonist training. The antagonist muscle works against the agonist, or primary movement muscle, to control the speed and direction of the force. If you watch someone doing a pull-up you'll see their triceps quiver a bit along the path of the pull-up as it assists in controlling it. Again, this is an extra workout exercise and is not meant to take the place of your main workout exercises.

Isolation is when you train a muscle completely out of context. If you do a standing shoulder press, your whole body and core work with the deltoid muscles to move, stabilize, and control the weight as it goes up and down. If you were to sit down in a lateral shoulder machine, you put your neck into the collar of the machine while sitting and then let your elbows go up and down with the weight. Your body is taken almost completely out of the movement and it's almost entirely deltoid muscles that do the work. There is a time and place for isolation, like rehab and therapy, but in general we should focus on compound movements.

Compound movement is when a lot of different muscle groups work together to move the weight. As in the above example the more of your body that is supporting the weight as it moves, the more bang for the buck you'll get in strength and fat loss. Deadlifts, squats, bench presses, standing shoulder presses, pull-ups, etc. are all great compound movements with a long history of training success.

Unilateral refers to an exercise that is performed with only one side at a time. A Unilateral Biceps Curl would be holding a dumbbell with one hand and lifting and lowering it for the reps to complete your set. Normally then you'd do a set with the other hand. In general I like unilateral movements because it's easier to concentrate on the motion more fully, which for some people yields faster results. Additionally you will be taxing the stabilizer muscles of the core for some benefit there.

Overcompensation training is when you train harder than you will have to perform. It can be as simple as a dad who has to carry around a 15 pound baby all night doing biceps curls with 30 pounds. Several people have asked about overcompensation for events, but if you look into it, most marathon runners do not train by running 30 miles. The negative effects would probably outweigh any benefit. They instead run slowly for time, rather than miles. Or run quickly for short distances. They gain training effect either way without unacceptable risk of injury or undue fatigue. They never run all-out for any length of time unless they're in a race. There are lots of ways to overcompensate without breaking.

If that all seems too complicated and confusing, let me simplify it somewhat. Do not think that if your Fourteener Performance Goal is a 1 MPH pace on a 6 mile hike with a 3000' elevation gain, you will need to train at 2 MPH for 12 miles with 6000' of elevation gain. There aren't enough benefits to that type of training to make it worth your while. The risk of overtraining and injury are too great. Especially if you're in the early stages of your training life.

Overtraining is when your workouts add up over time to be more than you can recover fully from in the time given. Some people can do 20 miles on a treadmill every week, at 4 miles a day 5 days in a row. Great. Others can only do 3 miles for 5 days a week. Others can do 7 miles every other day. You need to monitor yourself and know when you really are at the edge of injury or quitting as opposed to when you're just tired and worn out, but still able to do the next three workouts. It's a fine line to walk when you're training at your limit. Be aware. Best of all be self-aware. Skipping one workout to recover enough to do your next three workouts is a wise investment of recovery time. Missing three workouts because you forced yourself to do one today is a poor investment of training time.

Active Recovery is when you perform some other type of exercise or activity that is possibly just plain fun and has nothing directly to do with your chosen sport. An example could be a marathon runner roller skating with her kids. Sand volleyball, skiing, surfing - all could be fun active recovery options. Additionally, the "fun" aspect will be a break for your mind.

Failure is just what it sounds like. If you lift a weight 8 times with decent form then can't lift it the 9th time, you hit failure on the 9th rep. In my Training Journal I write that as 9F. That being said, I don't want you to hit failure on any of your workouts after the first few weeks of figuring out your own capacity for training.

Time format - in this program I'll use a standard USA time format.

0:30 = 30 seconds

1:30 = 1 minute and 30 seconds

2:05:10 = 2 hours, 5 minutes and 10 seconds

Selectorized Machine - a weight, strength, or functional training machine with a stack of weight plates into which you slide a pin in a numbered hole to set the resistance of the exercise. There are a few that use twisting knobs or sliders or other types of resistance settings. Typically the number on the weight stack and the actual weight at the end of the cables or handles are not the same. Some machines use numbers that imply weights (20, 30, 40, etc.). Some have simple numbers for how many plates you're lifting (1, 2, 3, etc.). Some even have a little conversion chart attached (4 = 18 lb.). Since you're not training to lift weights in a competition the exact pound weight isn't as important as keeping track of what you actually do during your workout. See the journaling chapter for more information.

Wrap Up - As I said, that's probably way more complicated than it needed to be, but some people will get hung up on it and some won't so I shot for the lowest common denominator. Some of these are merely presented to illustrate the concept for you in case you are interested in what I'm having you do, or what to take it further. If you're watching YouTube videos and reading articles on bodybuilding, fitness, or powerlifting websites, you might see some discrepancy between my definitions and theirs. Go with the flow. That means when you're in my book follow my definitions. When you're in their media, follow theirs. If it's going to drive you nuts leave comments on my Facebook. Thanks.

Stretching

Hiking up a Fourteener doesn't require any great amount of flexibility or mobility. If you can walk up a flight of stairs without pulling a muscle you should be fine. Various types of stretching, including Yoga and Tai Chi have thousands of years of history behind them. The benefits of stretching could include reduced muscle soreness, greater range of motion, faster recovery from training, and a general feeling of wellbeing.

On the flip side, there have been some studies lately showing that stretching is a very bad thing to do. You'll end up hurting yourself. You'll also become weaker and slower.

In response to the last claim I think that none of us are going to be running 6:00 miles or squatting with twice our bodyweight on the bar. Maybe I'm wrong, and if you are doing these things, then by all means, do your own study and make an informed decision as to whether you should or should not stretch. But for the rest of us, if our treadmill hikes at a 45:00 pace end up being 45:15 after a bit of stretching it's not going to really affect us in the big scheme of things. Similarly, if we're doing front shoulder raises at 8 pounds and stretching forces us down to 5 pounds it's not a big deal.

I myself do stretch on a regular basis and have for several years. Several like over 30. If you're already doing Yoga, Pilates, Tai Chi or any martial arts, you probably already know what to do, when and how. For those that don't stretch and want to learn how, I will show you one of the simple stretching routines I used to teach in a "Stretching for the Elderly" class at a Midwestern recreation center. As far as the hurting yourself claim I believe that if you move slowly and in control while doing static stretches you should be fine. Do not go all "Type A" on me here. It's not a competition to see who stretches the most the fastest. No bouncing and no extreme postures should be good enough to keep the average participant safe enough.

For this manual I'm presenting a short series of primarily dynamic warm-up stretches with a few static stretches thrown in. There are photos to help you understand them, and on the website link given previously you can find a video of all of them in a row. You can do them in about 5:00 – 10:00 minutes before every training session.

Training to Hike

What is hiking, when you get down to it? I'll suggest that hiking is walking on a rough surface that is steep in spots, and might require you to lean on trekking poles, or a tree, or a rock every now and again. For the 14ers you might have to step from rock to rock, somewhat like climbing stairs. You might also have to walk on snow, especially near the top in early summer. What skill is the most important for hiking as I've defined it? Walking. Plain and simple. Walking at an incline is probably the best overall training for hiking a 14er. I like to mix it up though, and using a stair or step machine can be great for the steeper and slower sections of trail. An elliptical or Arc trainer can help to avoid some types of injury from possible overtraining, and some of them can be adjusted to more accurately simulate an incline.

You should be hiking your 14er with trekking poles, which will require a little bit of upper body work for the back muscles, arm muscles, and chest muscles. Not a lot though, since trekking poles don't weigh all that much. You'll also need your core to be strong so that if you do slip and support yourself on your poles for a second you'll have the strength to get back into balance and keep walking. You will not be doing pull-ups on your trekking poles on the way up your mountain. At least we will hope not.

I like to add in some core work and strength training mostly to help avoid injury and provide a solid foundation for your hiking. It will also help you recover faster from your big adventure at the end of the program. Since this program starts "on the couch" and has a definite end goal, I won't spend a lot of time on other types of training or programs. If you are starting from a different background (not the couch – so you already train or work out on a regular basis) you can adjust these up a notch or two. I'm assuming that if you have been training for a while you will have a good idea on how to do that, so I won't be explaining all the variations of each exercise from the perspective of an advanced trainer.

One issue with the advanced trainer is that sometimes they have lost sight of their goals. They go in, work out, go home and might not be making any progress. Without a goal to compare your workout to, or base your workout on, sometimes you think you're making progress and you're not. Without fully understanding the requirements of your goal you might be doing some training that is actually detrimental to your goal. Sometimes it's as simple as just wasting your limited training time on conflicting goals.

If your goal is to climb a Fourteener, or do a big day hike, or whatever it is, and you only have an hour a day to train, then you shouldn't be spending that hour maxing out your bench press or biceps curls. You shouldn't be spending that hour a day doing Olympic style lifts. You can only be at your best on one goal at a time. If you're an advanced trainer you probably are not doing some of the exercises in this program. Set aside your other lifts for now and try these.

Try some variation on these. As an advanced trainer you probably have a really good idea what would work best on your chest or upper back and switch to a more endurance oriented approach to it. Just don't max out, okay?

Remember that it might be great for your body to change things up for a while. After your mountain is behind you then you can return to your old program with a fresh mind and body.

Establish your own training capacity and level

If you train with a heart rate monitor it could be pretty simple. Your watch probably has software that gives you some type of training zones and tells you which zone you're in, and whether it's time to take it easy or work harder. If you don't already have a watch like this, and can possibly find a way to afford one, I really suggest you get something in the mid–range price (or better) from your favorite manufacturer. I've had bad experiences with the low–end models from several of the major brands. The high–end models have functions and features that might not be all the important to you. Especially if you're just starting out. Unless you're doing a lot of your training outside, the GPS won't be very useful to you. One thing to consider is that several different online services have apps to record your routes and times, and some of them allow you to use the appropriate Bluetooth or ANT+ Heart Rate Belt.

If you're wanting to train using your pulse as a guideline, and are going without the software, the old formula was that your Max Heart Rate could be determined by subtracting your age from 220. This had a few flaws that affected primarily the older and younger people in a group, so it's been revised. Now use Maximum heart rate = 208 − (0.7 x age in years). In general, you will try your best to never train with your heart at this rate, especially as a beginner. As I mentioned before, you can take expensive tests from a clinic to get a more accurate number, but for the bulk of you the above formula is probably good enough. We're going to build in a safety buffer. Multiply this number by 0.8, by 0.7 and by 0.6. Memorize these resulting numbers. Put them in a whiteboard or poster by your training equipment. Tattoo them on your wrist. Just kidding!

Here's an example. If a 40 year old were to take the program:

$$208 - (0.7 \times 40) = 180$$

$$180 \times 0.8 = 144$$

$$180 \times 0.7 = 126$$

$$180 \times 0.6 = 108$$

Do the math for yourself and use the numbers you get. The .8x number (in the example 144) is the maximum effort I want you to exert during your training for the next several weeks. If you go over this number for more than a few seconds during any of your training in that period, drop your exertion level a lot until it drops down to the .6x number. Near the end of the program we'll see what happens if you do intervals with a heart rate greater than that.

The .7x number (in the example 126) is the lowest level of exertion I want you to train at. If during normal cardio training your heart rate drops below this number for more than a few seconds, then crank up the effort until it stays somewhere between the .7x and .8x numbers you get.

The last number is your resting, or warm-up level limit. If I call for a rest, or pause, or low interval, whatever a relative rest equates to, it's over when your heart rate drops below that number. This level is also good for a very long slow recovery session. If I call for a "warm-up" period, you need to keep your heart rate just above that 0.6x number – but by no means above the 0.7x number. I hope that's clear. I will try to be specific during the program.

Resting Zone = Descending heart rate until it reaches the 0.6x

Warm-up Zone = Stable heart rate between 0.6x and 0.7x

Training Zone = Heart Rate between 0.7x and 0.8x

Intensity Zone = Heart Rate greater than 0.8x

I'm not a fan of intervals at any intensity at the early levels of training. I will not ask you to enter the Intensity Zone. It's typically not necessary to complete a 14er. In general, if you do a workout in the Training Zone and stop, you should hit the Warm-up Zone in only a minute or so. If it takes longer than that make a note in your training journal and shoot for a lower heart rate the next session. You should be in the Resting Zone just a couple minutes after that. With more and more training over several weeks this recovery should become quicker. It's a normal effect of training.

For most people, a decent heart rate monitor, whether a phone app or watch, is an essential item to accurately track your own training progress. If you feel like you can't afford it, keep in mind that many of the phone apps are free, and the heart rate belt is less than $70. A decent enough watch should be under $130. Consider it a long term investment in your health and wellbeing for the rest of your life. Make a few small sacrifices now to reap many huge benefits later. If you can't get a heart rate monitor for one reason or other, quite a few cardio training machines have some type of handle grip with a heart rate readout, but most of them that I've used are about two minutes slow to report changes. In this program that can cause a few minor issues, especially in the 4 week adjustment cycle. A last resort is the **conversation method:**

Rest Zone/Warm-up Zone = full conversation with only a pause or two now and then

Training Zone = 3 to 4 word bursts with brief pauses

Intensity Zone = single word conversation mode with longer pauses

Go ahead, talk to yourself. No one will notice. Or at least they'll be too afraid to say anything to you about it.

Hanging On - if you have to hang on to the equipment rails or handlebars to prevent falling off, that may or may not be significant. One way to reduce your heart rate if it goes over is to quickly hang on. Normally your heart rate will drop by about 10 BPM in a few seconds. If you're hanging on and your heart rate goes too low, then let go and it should go up again soon. I have mixed feelings about hanging on. On the one hand it would be better for helping you build up your balance and stabilizer muscles if you don't hang on too much. On the other you'll be using trekking poles on the hike, so you'll be doing a bit of hanging on anyway during your big hike. If you absolutely have to hang on in order to get the workout session in with an acceptable speed goal, it would be okay I guess. I'd rather you didn't though. If you want to try to break the "hanging on habit" I recommend that you hold two 3 lb. dumbbells, one in each hand. Sometimes just having something in your hands will do the trick to break the habit. Break in gently if you need to, with only one and switch hands every few minutes.

Fat Loss

There is one two-edged sword to this program. You might lose fat. You might not lose fat. Sorry, but this is a program designed to build the type of fitness you need to climb a mountain. It's a long slog to the top, and our only performance goals relate to the number of feet you can ascend in an hour. We're working at a relatively low heart rate, since in the actual climb you don't want your heart rate to go so high that you crash and burn. The sad fact of high heart rates is that there's only so much fuel in the tank. Without a lengthy physiological explanation, think of it like fuel in a car. On idle your gallon of gas will last hours. Floor the throttle and that gallon of gas might be gone in a few minutes.

Training at this level of exertion might result in fat loss for some people. For others it might not. I don't know anything about your metabolism, so I make no promises in regard to fat loss. There are no dietary elements to this plan. It's hard sometimes to have two single most important things in the world to accomplish. If your primary goal is fat loss, all I can say is to please set that aside for now. Train to climb the mountain. If you also eat in a way that results in fat loss at the same time, then good for you. Congratulations. I mean it. It's hard to do two things very well at the same time.

Once you've achieved your mountaineering goal then you can re-assess your priorities. It's easier to maintain a level of fitness than it is to earn it in the first place. After your summit you can step back a bit in the long duration endurance training and crank up some fat burning style training for a while. If you see a mountaineering objective coming up, about 6 weeks out you can switch back to endurance training as you prepare for your next summit. If you train in cycles like this it will have the best long-term effect on your fitness, body composition, and athletic performance.

Photo, next page: Recent photo of myself at 185 pounds after a 5K PR

Summit Success

Cardio Tools

I prefer things to be as simple as possible. I hope I don't make it sound like you need some special tools, or gear, or equipment or machines. If you belong to a club or gym or recreation center, great. If not, great. I will admit that for some of you getting in enough vertical in a week without some form of cardio machine might be tough, but we'll do our best to work around that.

If you don't have any machinery or equipment to work with, you'll have to work with walking with a backpack on roads, trails, and stairs. It might be tough to find these, or maybe not. If you're motivated you'll figure it out.

If you have access to a fitness center, or by some chance happen to own machinery, these are my preferred pieces of cardio equipment:

Treadmill – many standard motorized treadmills allow you to adjust the angle. The number refers to % of inclination generally. 1% means 1 foot of elevation at the end of a 100 foot ramp. 12% is 12 feet up at the end of 100 feet. Some very steep trails go up to 40% or more, though on average, the simpler 14ers rarely go beyond 24% for very long. Many treadmills go up to 12 to 15%. There are special Incline Treadmills that go in the 40% range. These are great if you have access to them, though I plan on getting you there without having to use anything beyond the 15% range. It's up to you. Adjust the plan based on your heart rate zone if you decide to go for more inclination. This usually ends up being about 1/2 the speed you would use at 15%. Some of them report your vertical gain during a workout, and after testing a few models they seem to be within a percent or two of reality. Don't trust it 100% though. Use the calculator.

Elliptical – I used to use an elliptical almost every day that I didn't train outside. Some ellipticals have a vertically sliding front plate, or have the swing arms for the legs hinged in such a way that it can mimic a vertical step more closely. The Cybex ARC trainer is one with the hinged arms. If you adjust it right you can actually move somewhat like cross country skiing uphill. If you have access to one, definitely use it. When I had access to one I used it every day and used the vertical feet reading on the console to plan my workouts. I include ellipticals now primarily as cross-training machines, during the main part of the program.

Stair Machines – there are two types of stair machines. One has foot plates that slide up and down and slightly forward in a track or on swing arms. The other is the Stepmill - like a treadmill with steps on it, tilted at a 45 degree angle. I prefer the Stepmill, but the other is fine too. If you can use one, use it with a pack and be sure you know your "weight with pack" every time, because you enter that for the machine to set your resistance. My Stepmill Calculator was written for the Stepmill. I measured the stair treads to develop the math for it. The math will not be correct for a stepper machine. The foot pad angles are not the same as on the Stepmill. The stepper machine will also let you determine the distance you move each foot so it won't add up the same as on the Stepmill, on which that next step is coming and will always be the same height to step up onto. If the stepper machine you're using has a readout of Vertical Feet then you can keep track of it to develop your own pace to work toward the Fourteener goals we're going to establish. Hopefully it is accurate enough to work out in the long run.

Stairs, Steps, and Boxes – there is so much you can do with a simple set of boxes, flight of stairs, or even a park bench or flower bed wall to step up onto and back off from. If you want to use your poles for balance that would be acceptable if it's not on a gym floor. Though I wouldn't recommend doing it in any stairway, even cement. If you scratch the floor you might ruin a good thing for a lot of people. I have a set of poles for indoor use with a rubber knob fit over the end to cushion the point and reduce damage.

No matter what machine you do use, keep in mind that a great way to get injured in a hurry is to slam your feet, especially your heels, into the deck or stairs or foot pads. It's even worse if your knees are pretty straight, straight, or even more than straight (hyper extended is the term). You need to keep your joints flexed and stable enough to control your motion and speed safely, but soft enough to prevent injury. This is a serious warning to take it to heart and make sure you use your gear safely.

Photo, next page, is an elliptical and incline treadmill in an insulated garage. One of the best investments in my health and fitness and well worth the money.

Training for Hiking, Mountaineering, and Peak Bagging – by Charles Miske

Machines to avoid for your base cardio training

Anything "as-seen-on-TV"

Jacob's Ladder – unless you've been using one for at least a month or more. Don't start now. The motion isn't like anything you'll be using on a standard summer climb of one of the easier 14ers. If you have been using one now and then, it would be okay to put it into your cross-training days. From a specificity point of view it would be great training for low angle mixed, ice, or snow climbing. If you become an advanced Fourteener climber this might be a fun goal.

Skiing Machines - I do like them a bit. If you already know how to use one of the old-school cross country ski machines then you can do this on your cross-training days. Otherwise it's not worth learning right now. You have enough to worry about.

Rowing Machines are a great workout and I myself spent a lot of time on one in the earlier days of my training. But I was training for Ice Climbing endurance as well. If I were training only for hiking a 14er I would have avoided it.

Cycles of any type, stationary, recumbent, spinning, anything with pedals and a wheel of some type. It's not directly applicable to hiking a 14er for most people unless you're at a relatively high level of training. That being said a very long time ago one of my first bigger mountains was Timpanogos in Utah as a Boy Scout leader and at the time I was a bicycle commuter riding 28 miles round trip 4 days a week with an additional 2 days a week of moderate strength training. My group of boys was among the first to the top of the 11, 750' mountain after 5,000' of ascent from the trailhead. So save it for cross training, if at all.

Climbing Machines like the Versa Climber or a climbing treadwall. Great cardio and cross training, but not applicable to this program. They would be fine for Ice Climbing or Rock Climbing training with excellent specificity.

Online Cardio Tools

I made some calculators for you on my website.

One is a Stairmaster Stepmill Calculator. Plug in your Steps per Minute (use the Average from the console readout if you changed it during your training session) and duration in 00:00 format (no seconds) and you'll get your vertical feet, actual miles, and various speeds.

The other is an Incline Treadmill Calculator. You plug in your incline percentage, your total miles, and total time in 00:00 format (no seconds). You'll get the same information as in the Stepmill Calculator. It also works for a standard treadmill, only you'll probably never type in more than 15%, which is the normal maximum for an average treadmill like you'd find in a fitness center, recreation center, or gym.

Be sure to keep track of this information in your training journal. It will be very important to plan your own progress and help you achieve your goals. Once more, I strongly advocate measuring everything you do to ensure that you are in fact sticking to the plan, achieving your goals, and making the progress you need to make.

Here is a link to where you can find these calculators:

http://sevensummitsbody.com/summitsuccess

Strength Training Tools

I prefer using the word strength to the word weights in this program. I don't think you absolutely have to use any weight other than your backpack or bodyweight at the beginning level. I have a few simple exercises to do on the Strength Days.

For current strength trainers. If you're already doing weights at any level, I need you to seriously consider how important it is in the context of your goal of doing a 14er. I need you to be fully recovered and ready to train on your cardio days. Those sessions are way more important in this program. If you are limping for a week after your squat training, that's not going to work with this program. Sorry. I'm not saying you "can't" do it – just adjust your level some to accommodate this program. As I stated previously, it's not too hard to maintain a level of fitness for several weeks without appreciable losses. After you get your summit you can go right back into it, and your muscles will be fresh and ready to rock it after your little period of reduced intensity. Your body might even thank you for the break by giving you even faster gains after this period of relative rest.

Home Style Strength Training Equipment

You won't need all of these. You might be able to figure out a substitute. You could consolidate and do the whole thing with or without any of these. Even do them all with one of these. Here are some of the small tools I recommend:

Straps – TRX, Blast Straps, whatever. It's all the same really. Some nylon webbing with handles and some type of clips or clamps. There was a fad a couple years ago, and a lot of gyms have some variation on these. If not, you can get them for fairly cheap, or make them for even cheaper.

Bands – rubber tubing by Jump Stretch, EliteFTS or others. Try to avoid the cheap rubber tubes sold by discount chain stores including the big sports stores. They will break if you crank on them. You will only need the lightest/thinnest ones for this program. Lightest/thinnest is of course relative. *Light* to a bodybuilder or power lifter is different from *light* to a yoga or Pilate's class.

Small Hand Weights – seriously, small bags of rice will do the trick. If you have access to them, 3 and 5 pound weights are handy. The 1 pound size is about right for assisting in cardio training to simulate carrying trekking poles. Don't worry about what you look like. If you're at a gym they'll have weights. You won't have to do your workout using a can of beans for hand weights in front of people.

Benches – chairs, stools, stairs, ladders, step-stools – anything you feel comfortable stepping up and down on. Or sitting on. It has to support your weight on one foot without wobbling or feeling like it will fall apart. Most gyms will have stacking metal frame boxes. I like these a lot. At home you'll have to be creative. Once you see what it is you have to do, you can look around to make it work.

Mat – the thick carpets like you place in front of your kitchen sink will do the trick. Some gyms make you bring your own mats. Some have a bin of mats hidden in the yoga or cardio room.

Gym Style Strength Training Equipment

If you can get to a gym of any type, you'll probably find a pretty broad spectrum of equipment. Free weights, machines, functional trainers, various stools and benches and platforms are all widely available in most gyms. If you haven't used them all, see if your gym offers a free orientation session. Some do them as group sessions a few times a week. Get the instructor to make sure you know how to use everything. I can show you how to do all of the exercises in this book a few different ways, but I can't promise you'll have that exact same combination of equipment. If possible, the more different machines you know how to use, the better it will be for adjusting my program to suit your conditions.

The simplest most basic strength training tools you can use in a gym, above and beyond those already listed, would be dumbbells. If you have access to a set of dumbbells that go from 10-30 pounds that would be great. Most people coming off the couch and doing this program shouldn't need any more weight than that. If you have kettle bells in that weight range, that's fine too.

If you're a more advanced trainer, you will be able to use barbells for some of the exercises in this program. I'll touch on that briefly in some of the examples. If you're not currently able to do a Deadlift, squat, or bench press with a bar set at your own bodyweight, then for right now just follow the program until you find out how your own strength fits into it. Then you can make adjustments as needed. If it's just not working for you, contact me on the blog and I'll see if I can find a way to help you.

No matter what type of equipment you end up using for your strength training, you must know how to use it safely. If you are in a commercial facility or other training club, be sure to get checked out on the equipment. If you're using your own tools in your own home, then please read the directions and warnings. You can easily hit yourself with anything that moves, stretches, or pulls. You can hurt yourself standing up from a squat and hitting a doorway. Make sure your training area is safe for yourself and others, and please don't go too far, too fast, too strong, out of control or otherwise pose a hazard to yourself or others. Thanks!

Photo, next page is a collection of gym style equipment including barbells, racks, and benches - but in a home setting. It's not as expensive as you might think and was one of the best investments I ever made in my health and fitness.

Training for Hiking, Mountaineering, and Peak Bagging – by Charles Miske

Journaling

Journaling is very important in this program. In my opinion, journaling is essential to progress in any program. Journaling is how we keep track of our daily performance, our daily goals, and our daily success. There is an old saying:

IF YOU CAN'T MEASURE IT YOU CAN'T MANAGE IT.

You might have caught on by now that this is very important to me. I've been keeping a training journal for over 5 years. I can plan workouts based on old workouts and I know what I can do on dozens of different equipment variations.

Your journal itself can be in just about anything. I've used one of those little black-and-white-marble covered composition books. I've used a little whiteboard and washable marker combination, and it was one of my favorite ways to journal for years. I got it in the Dollar Bins just inside Target four years ago. Recently, when training in a recreation center, I've been using Color Note, a phone app, to write my training journal in. When I was done logging my day in my whiteboard I would then type it into a private blog I share with my wife so we could compare notes and goals and check each other for accountability. Having someone to check up on you as an accountability partner is another secret trick to speeding up your success. I highly recommend it.

Strength Training Journaling Examples

I want you to record everything you do for your strength training. If you use a weight machine, record exactly what it says. If it has LB or pounds or Kg or some other markings, use that, otherwise use the Level number from the machine or stacks of plates or whatever it uses for resistance. Here are a few examples showing how I record workouts:

Exercise: Reps @ weight or level x sets

The exercise name, then the number of reps I did, then the resistance, either the weight or level number, then the number of sets.

Gravitron: 25 @ -90 Lb.

To explain that one, it's the Gravitron Machine which is an assisted pull-up machine. It subtracts weight from your bodyweight when you use it to do your exercises. It's a selectorized machine with the plates labeled in pounds. In this case I'm doing 25 reps with 90 pounds of assistance.

Cable Chest Fly: 10 @ L4 each x 3

This one is a cable chest fly, which is usually a selectorized machine with two weight stacks about 8' apart attached to adjustable pulleys and handles. This journal entry shows 3 sets of 10 reps with both weight stacks set at level 4. Here's is an alternate view of the "each" thing.

Triceps Rope Press: 10 each @ L3 x 3

That's 3 sets of 10 reps using one hand at a time, alternated, at level 3. That's how I use "each" in a journal entry. If I put the each after the rep count, I mean that I've done it one side at a time. If I put it after the weight that means that I've done both sides with separate weights, like with dumbbells or weight stacks on a machine. Now for a more conventional free weight exercise.

Deadlift: 10 @ 90 / 155 x 10 fast

This is the classic Deadlift compound movement. In this example I do 10 reps at 90 pounds (the bar is 45 pounds + 45 pounds of weight, which is 2 x 10 Kg plates = close enough). The slash "/" indicates I'm using the same count (10) but different weight. I added 2 more plates then to equal 155 pounds and did 10 more sets. I added the note "fast" to the end to indicate that I did this exercise relatively quickly. The 10 x 10 protocol can have excellent endurance and metabolic effects for an advanced trainer.

Bent Over Row: 25 @ 45 Lb.; 5 @ 145 Lb. x 5

In this example I'm switching weight and counts, so I separate the journal entry with a semicolon ";" to indicate that there is new and different data in the entry. I'm doing a bent over row back exercise. First I do a set of 25 reps at 45 pounds and then do 5 sets of 5 at 145 pounds.

I hope that these simple examples are enough to help you get started on your own training journal. These notations have been developed over the 5 years of my own training journals. They're based on ease of writing them while you're panting and out of breath between sets. They're based on readability for when you transfer them to an online journal later, or want to read them in a couple years to see how much progress you've made.

Cardio Training Journaling Examples

Again, I want you to record everything exactly as it happens on your cardio machine. The console or monitor on the machine you use will tell you everything you need to know, in general. One gotcha is that sometimes the machine will display something different at the end of your workout that might not include the information you need. While on the machine you might get miles and feet and average heart rate and speeds and vertical feet. When you stop the machine to get off it might wave some flags and toot some horns and tell you that you did 358 METS (whatever that means) and there's no way to get to the data you really need. If you find that to be the case, you can slow the machine down to a crawl or pause it before you get off, and still get all the right info. Some machines will also just stop themselves if you step off or stop moving your feet. Sometimes you lose your workout data, sometimes you don't.

Example from a Treadmill Workout

Treadmill: 24:00 - .67 mi - 12%

That's from doing 24 minutes on a treadmill at 12% incline ending up with .67 miles. That's the quick notation from the console. Always get that first before the machine resets the console. If you plug that into my Incline Treadmill Calculator you end up with the following:

Incline Treadmill Calculator Display

Time: 24:00

Distance: .67

Incline: 12%

Elevation Gain: 424.51'

Average MPH: 1.675

Average Pace: 35:49

Vertical/Hour: 1061'

Vertical/Minute: 17.69'

VAM: 323.5

I'd like for you to put that information in your journal for every treadmill workout, in addition to the initial note from the screen right after your workout. That has a lot of extremely helpful information. A thousand feet of vertical in an hour is excellent and great training for a successful 14er climb.

Example from a Stairmaster Stepmill Workout.

Stepmill: 30:00 - 25 SPM (ave.) - 47 floors - 1.1 miles

Not much there, right? The Stepmill will also tell you how many floors you did, and how many miles you walked. The miles are nowhere near correct by any type of math you could dream up. I could explain it to you if you're interested. I measured it for the calculator. Trust the calculator. Some models tell you METS, some tell you Watts. So in my opinion, you can record the floors and miles just for your own comparison from workout to workout to see if you're making progress, but don't get hung up over them. SPM is your Steps-Per-Minute. I used (ave.) in this example because I got that off the display as my average SPM. If I were to have just set it at 25 and used that the whole time I would not have added in the (ave.). If you go up and down in speed, at the end the display will let you know your average SPM. If you plug that data into my Stepmill Calculator you get the following.

Stepmill Calculator Display

Time: 30:00

Steps/Minute: 25

Vertical Feet: 500.00

Miles: 0.11

Average MPH: 0.213

Average Pace: 281:36

Vertical/Hour: 1000.00

Vertical/Minute: 16.67

VAM: 304.8

As you can see, the miles are quite a bit different from the console. These numbers are arrived at using math from actually measuring the size of the steps and calculating the total forward movement. As you can see from this example, we got 1000' per hour of upward movement. Again, a good workout for your Fourteener hike coming up. Put that info in your Training Journal. It will be great to compare it with your past and future workouts to monitor your progress.

Now for an example from outside training. If you use an online phone app like Strava, Map-MyRun or something similar, or if you use a heart rate watch with a GPS there should be a screen in the device (watch/phone) or an online workout display to copy your stats from. Here is an example of an outside training session.

Snowshoe: 1:07:10, 3.34 mi, 3.0 MPH (ave), +299'/-322', 136 BPM HR (ave)

That's a 5K on snowshoes, approximately a half hour each way up and down a moderately steep trail in Colorado. In about a half hour I gained 300'. I lost more feet on the way down because I stopped in a different location from where I started. 600' per hour is on the low side of where we want to be for our upcoming Fourteener trip, but then 3.0 mph is faster than we need to be, so it evens out a bit. In any case, with the soft snow it was a great workout. I got this data from the website my training watch synchronizes with. Yours might vary a bit. For your journal just get the important info in there.

This brings up a great point to consider. Training outside is much more variable because it's fairly hard to find a good long stretch of 15% incline or greater to train on. You might have to go a bit faster on shallower ground, or go more miles, to make up your vertical goals. Once you know and understand your own body and how it will react to training, and more importantly, a 14er, then you can work on your own style and quantity of training that will get you to the top. By then you'll be an advanced trainer and hopefully have the tools you need to develop your own training program.

The calculators I programmed or this training program can be found at

http://sevensummitsbody.com/summitsuccess

Please bookmark the page that applies to you, either for the Treadmill or the Stepmill or both.

Light Stretching for Cardio and Strength Training

At the beginning of each Cardio and Strength Training Session I'd like you to spend about 8:00 (eight minutes) doing some light dynamic stretching. I want you to hang onto something for balance, as most of these require you to be on one leg moving and I don't want you to be injured by a loss of balance. For extra fun and some level of specificity, use your poles for balance. I have also included a few optional static stretches, if you're interested and inclined. You do not have to do the static stretches unless you want to.

Some of the dynamic stretches are dependent on your sense of balance. I recommend you use your trekking poles if you need to. They add in some specificity and help a lot to support you while you learn balance. Just don't lean on them too heavily or if your hands slip you might take a hard fall. Remember, specificity is how closely your training resembles the activity you're training for. Supporting your weight somewhat for balance on your poles will be among your activities.

After the static stretching then we move to the upper body stretching. I created a video demonstration of all of the stretches listed here and it took a little less than 10:00. If you go to http://sevensummitsbody.com/summitsuccess you'll find links to that video and lots of other free goodies. Check it out if you're having difficulties figuring out what the descriptions here refer to.

Knee Up, Heel Back

Keeping your back somewhat upright and neutral bring your knee up toward your chest and then kick your heel back behind you. Repeat a dozen or so times on each side. Avoid the impulse to extend your range of motion to the rear by leaning forward.

Leg Swing

Similar to the above, but with a nearly straight knee. Go ahead and give this one a little body English, leaning to the front to both lean toward your toes when they are to the front, and to reach further back with your heel. It's just big swings front and rear. Switch sides and repeat.

Summit Success

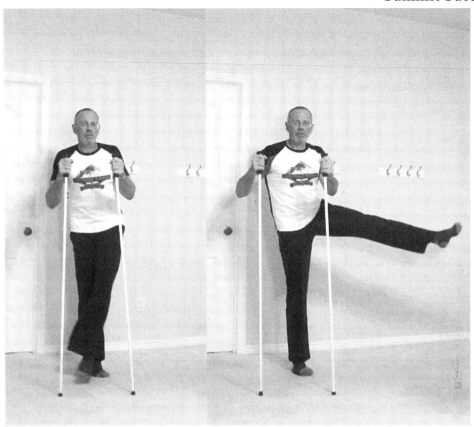

Sideways Leg Swing

Similar to the above Leg Swing, but to the side. If you're using trekking poles set them on the opposite side and lean that way, away from the swinging leg. Cross the leg slightly to the front and then to the rear and alternate. Do not try really hard to reach for the maximum extension or try to hold it to the side. Just let it fly. Give it a dozen and then switch sides.

Forward Leaning Glute Swing

Now you can lean forward. Lean on your poles, keep your back arched with a good posture position, don't hunch your shoulders and reach your foot as high to the rear as possible. You can tilt your toes out a bit if that makes it feel better. Be sure to bail on this if you accidentally hunch your back and feel any discomfort. Again, a dozen each side.

Summit Success

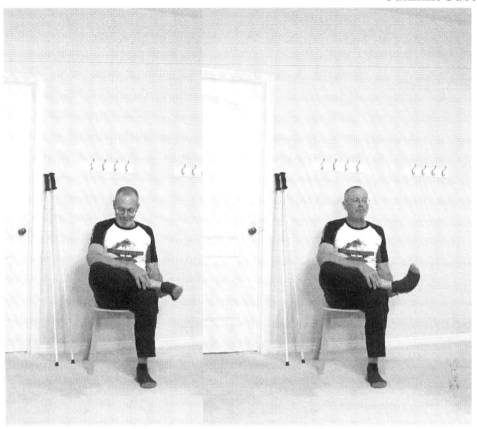

Sitting Toe Circles

Sit with one leg over the top of the other with your foot extended to the outside of your knee. With the point of your toe draw little smooth imaginary circles in the air. Go both ways about a dozen times. Switch feet and repeat.

Deep Squat Static Stretch

Only do this if you are pretty sure you can. That's a smooth way of saying it's not for everyone. Beware of any issues you have with knees, ankles or back. You can even tweak your shoulder doing this. Be aware, alert, and ready to bail.

Plant your feet about shoulder width apart, toes pointing out at 45 degrees. That's pointing 90 degrees away from each other. As you get more experience you can pick your own width and angles, but this is a good starting point.

Gently, carefully squat down, so that your bottom is down near your heels. Your elbows can go inside or outside your knees. I prefer inside. Keep your back arched properly, as in good posture. Only go down as far as your back keeps this arch. Your back will cue you in to the fact that you've gone too far for your own personal flexibility level by curving backward at the arch. Like curling your stomach up. You can video yourself if you want to check it.

One way to keep your back in the right position is to point your chin up and out a little. Just enough to keep your back straight. Hold the stretch for about 20 to 30 seconds tops. For most people not practicing martial arts or some other athletic endeavor that requires great flexibility this will be long enough.

Illustrated on following page.

Summit Success

Butterfly Static Stretch

I like to just drop down from the Squat Stretch. The point is to sit with your back straight. One way to keep your back straight is to point your chin up and out a little. Just enough to keep your back straight.

Set the soles of your feet together a couple feet out from you with your knees pretty much on the ground out to the side. It should look like a large diamond shape. Keep your back straight and gently bring your feet in closer to you with your hands if needed. When your back starts to reverse the curve or your knees come up more than a couple inches from the ground that's your limit. Bare feet or thin shoes work best.

Hold that for about 20 to 30 seconds and you're done. Illustrated on following page.

Hamstring Static Stretch

From the Butterfly Stretch carefully extend one leg to the front. Straight out or even 45 degrees to the side or anywhere in between is fine. Keeping your leg relatively straight and your back with a good posture arch, reach gently toward your extended foot with either hand. The same hand as the leg (IE Right-Right or Left-Left) should be easier. Don't reach way out by curving your back or chest or shoulders. When you hit the furthest you can go with good posture that's it. Hold for 20 to 30 seconds and you're good. Bring your foot in gently, switch to the other side and repeat.

If the back of your knees hurt when you reach then you can roll up a towel or small foam roller or little dumbbell under your knee to keep a bit of bend in it. You'll still get a stretch without quite so much pain in your knee. Like anything else, if you have real pain and can't get past it find out what's wrong and do something else.

Illustrated on following page.

Calf Static Stretch

Stand straight upright with your legs together and reach out behind you with one foot in a lunge position. Keep that foot flat on the floor as you gently press your navel toward the floor ahead of you while keeping your back arched in a proper posture position. Hold for about 20 seconds then come back to center under control and switch feet, extending the other foot to the rear. Be sure to point your toes straight ahead and don't reach so far back that your heel lifts on the rear foot. Support your weight on your front foot and use your hands on the front knee for support if you need it and are not using trekking poles to assist. Illustrated on following page.

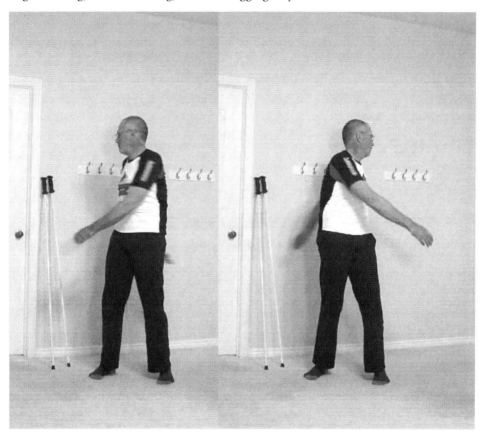

Arm Circles

Stand upright with legs about shoulder width apart or wider, toes pointed to the front. Twist your torso and shoulders and let your hands fly freely, gently slapping your sides at the end of the motion. Reverse and let your hands fly and slap the other side gently. Repeat about a dozen times.

Windmills Front and Rear

Standing with your feet together, take one arm and keeping it close to your side, lift it up to the front and over your head and to the rear in a large circle. Keep it moving freely within the limits of your shoulders and elbows. After about a dozen circles reverse the motion to lifting to the rear, up and over and down the front for a dozen. Switch sides and repeat.

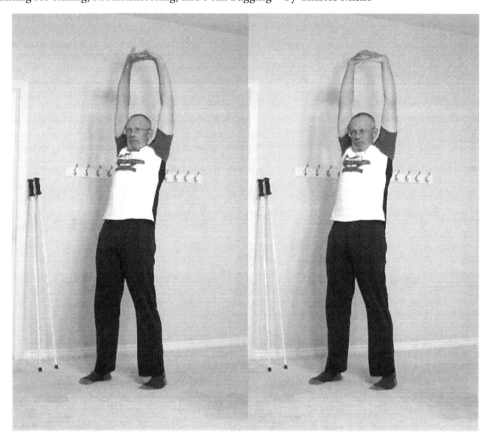

Ceiling to Floor Presses Palms In and Palms Out

Standing as above, lock your fingers together with your palms facing inward. Straighten your arms, pressing your knuckles toward the floor. Gently raise your arms to the front keeping your knuckles pointing outward. Your wrists should be sharply angled. At the top press your hands toward the ceiling and then reverse the motion back toward the floor.

Flip your hands over so that your fingers are locked and your palms face outward and press down toward the floor. Again raise your arms to the front so that your palms press toward the ceiling at the top. Hold for a second and then return toward the floor and press for a second.

Ceiling Press Lean and Floor Press Twist

Ceiling Press Lean:

Repeat the above with the palms out, and at the top lean over to the right as far as you can comfortably bend and then to the left. Hold for a few seconds at each extreme.

Floor Press Twists:

Continuing on from the above, at the bottom press toward the floor and turn your torso and shoulders and press toward the floor with your palms by the side of your leg. Repeat on the other side.

Training for Hiking, Mountaineering, and Peak Bagging – by Charles Miske

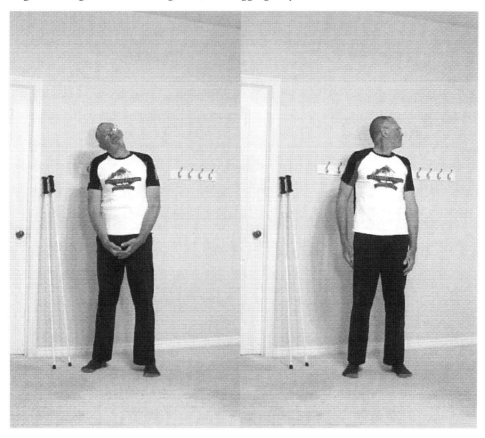

Neck Turn and Neck Tilt

Neck Turn:

Keeping your shoulders still, gently and slowly look from side to side over each shoulder about a dozen times each way.

Neck Tilt:

Again, keeping your shoulders still, and looking to the front, tilt your head down toward your shoulder being sure not to lift your shoulder to meet your neck. Tilt the other side and repeat about a dozen times.

The Dynamic and Static Stretches Outdoors

I'm going to take a few pages here to repeat the Dynamic and Static Stretches for you once again. This time done outside for a different view. One of the best things about this program is that even though it appears very structured (wait till you see the training charts) it's so variable in nature that you can do just about anything in it either inside or outside, in your home or a commercial gym or out in the trails.

In this sequence I'm standing outside near a river alongside a popular trail near the Keystone Ski Resort. It's where I created the video version that I made available to my 2014 training group subscribers. Now that the season is over I'm making it available to you. Again, just go to http://sevensummitsbody.com/summitsuccess and you'll find it listed in the contents available to you as a reader of this book.

Training for Hiking, Mountaineering, and Peak Bagging – by Charles Miske

Knee Up, Heel Back

Leg Swing

Training for Hiking, Mountaineering, and Peak Bagging – by Charles Miske

Sideways Leg Swing

Forward Leaning Glute Kick

Summit Success

Training for Hiking, Mountaineering, and Peak Bagging – by Charles Miske

Standing Toe Circles

Summit Success

Deep Squat and Butterfly Static Stretches

63

Training for Hiking, Mountaineering, and Peak Bagging – by Charles Miske

Hamstring Static Stretch

Calf Static Stretch

Training for Hiking, Mountaineering, and Peak Bagging – by Charles Miske

Arm Circles

Summit Success

Windmills Front and Rear

Training for Hiking, Mountaineering, and Peak Bagging – by Charles Miske

Ceiling to Floor Press

Summit Success

Ceiling Press Lean

Floor Press Twist

Summit Success

Neck Turn

71

Training for Hiking, Mountaineering, and Peak Bagging – by Charles Miske

Neck Tilt

Cardio Training for the First Four Weeks

This is your Adjustment Cycle. This is your General Physical Preparedness cycle. This is how you figure out what level you're at. If you're already a more advanced trainer you might skip this, but you might think it's pretty fun and cool to try at least a couple weeks of it, especially if you've never done any vertical training before.

If you truly are coming off the couch for this program, then please follow the guidelines very carefully. If you're a more advanced trainer then you probably have a really good idea at what levels you should stop, but remember, for this program we really want that heart rate to guide our training goals. For right now I don't want you to use any backpack or additional weights or other types of resistance. We'll add those in after the Adjustment Cycle is complete in four weeks.

In the assessments previously, I asked you to find out what types of equipment you would be able to use, some form of heart rate monitor, and the numbers for your heart rate zones. Primarily in this training cycle I want you use either a treadmill with a variable incline setting, or a stepper, preferably a stepmill. If you have access to both, I overall prefer that you do the steps one day a week, and then the treadmill on the other cardio training days you have available.

I want you to do 3 or 4 cardio training days each of the 4 weeks. I want you to do strength training 2 days a week. That adds up to either 5 or 6 days a week. If you can do 6 training days great, you will make better and faster progress in adapting to the steepness of the treadmill. Otherwise do 5. These early stages are a little different between the Stepmill and the treadmill. On the Stepmill the angle is predetermined and cannot be adjusted. The steps are horizontal and you get what you get and don't feel like you're slipping backward off the treadmill belt and you don't have the same stress on your calves unless you stay on the balls of your feet much of the time. With the treadmill at steep angles those are all problems and this first four weeks allows you to adjust to that somewhat.

I mentioned a time commitment for this program as well. This adjustment period is also to help you adjust to your time commitment for the remaining 12 weeks. I'm going to first give you your cardio training sessions for the 4 week cycle, followed by the strength training sessions.

You might want to wear very light synthetic shorts and top to allow for good ventilation and temperature control. If you're at home on your own machines it doesn't matter except comfort. I often use my cardio machines at home in just running shorts and shoes. Be aware of others around you and respect them. Wear clean clothes for each training session. Black has a tendency to show sweat a bit less than other colors. If you sweat a lot and will have soaked clothing bring something to change into right away. Especially in the later stages of your training when you might do weights and cardio in the same session.

If your hands get sweaty you can wear training or bike gloves. I like the extra grip they give on the handles of the machines too. You could wear terry wrist bands like baseball and tennis players so that your hands don't drip on the machine decks. Carry a couple of hand towels of cotton or microfiber to set over the hand rails of the machines. Use clean ones each time. Have one to wipe your face and head and upper chest. A lot of people who are new to training, especially if they consume caffeine regularly, will drip a lot until their body adjusts. This little section might sound gross, but it's essential to go in without the rose colored glasses. I don't want you to get embarrassed by not knowing how to deal with this and not want to set foot in the gym again.

Footwear for cardio depends on a lot. If you already have shoes that you use and love and want to keep using them, it's probably fine. If you have the hiking boots you'll use for the mountain at the end of the program, go ahead and use them. They should be fine for most of the machines. I have evolved over time and now like to use a pair of thin soled running shoes for most of my inside training except running on a treadmill when I prefer cushioned shoes for faster recovery. These are just ideas. You can make it work. Please don't go barefoot or in flip flops though. It's just too dangerous with a lot of moving parts.

If you're using a treadmill with a variable incline setting

Training Week	Target Vertical	Target Miles	Miles at 3%	Miles at 6%	Miles at 9%	Miles at 12%
1	824	3.59	5.20	2.60	1.73	1.30
2	915	3.95	5.78	2.89	1.93	1.44
3	1,017	4.34	6.42	3.21	2.14	1.60
4	1,130	4.78	7.13	3.57	2.38	1.78

I have two versions of the plan for the first four weeks, your Adjustment Cycle. I'll describe both versions for each of the weeks. When it's time for the Main Training Cycle, it will be as in the chart above. You'll be training for mileage and vertical foot of ascent goals. I want you to be conscious of your heart rate though, and not go into the hard effort zones. For many people that will cause conflicts with recovery and lead to reduced training efficiency.

Treadmill Basic Instructions

Set the incline to your target percentage. Set the speed at 1.0 MPH.

Warm Up: Stay at that speed for 3:00 to 5:00. If your heart rate goes into the Training Zone at any time during this warm-up, drop your speed by .1 MPH and repeat every 0:30 until your heart rate descends back into the Warm-up Zone. If you go below the Warm-up Zone then up the speed by .1 MPH every 0:30 until you're back in the middle of your Warm-up Zone.

Training: Bump the speed up by .2 MPH. Repeat every 1:30 until your heart rate is in the upper range of the Training Zone. Take a note of what that speed is. If your heart rate goes into the Intensity Zone drop down .2 MPH every 1:30 until you are back into the Training Zone. If your heart rate drops down into the Warm-up Zone then increase your speed by .2 MPH until you are back into the Training Zone. Keep your eyes on your heart rate. Keep this up until you have 3:00 to 5:00 remaining for your intended exercise time. If by some chance your heart rate doesn't get up into the Training Zone, and you end up getting frustrated and bump it up into the 4.0 MPH + range, then you are most likely sandbagging this and an advanced trainer. Skip ahead a week or two in the charts and hold there until the beginning of the main program.

Cool Down: Drop your speed by approximately 1/2. Hang on. Let your heart rate descend into the Warm-up Zone. If it goes down into the Resting Zone that's fine this for the Adjustment Cycle.

Journaling: Get your stats from the console and plug them into my Incline Treadmill Calculator. Keep track of this in your journal. You will need this information to plan out all of the upcoming workouts. Be sure to note the information from my calculator, your max speed, and how you felt. If you thought it was too easy, if you had to use your hands a lot or not at all. It's all important info.

Treadmill Math Example

When you're first starting out, with 824 feet as your weekly goal, and you decide to walk at 3% for four sessions of 24:00 (24 minutes) here is what the math would look like:

Week One Training From the chart:

824 at 3% = 5.20 miles

4 x 24 minutes = 96 minutes

96 minutes ÷ 60 minutes/hour = 1.60 hours

5.20 miles ÷ 1.60 hours = 3.25 mph

Since most treadmills can't be set for 3.25 you can do one of three things.

1. Go over – set your speed to 3.3 mph and go with that.
2. Average – go at 3.3 mph for half, and 3.2 mph for half.
3. Just go for distance – 5.20 ÷ 4 = 1.3 miles per day.

I'm including this in case you're curious how I derived my numbers and in case you want to generate your very own custom program. So long as you make the bulk of the program revolve around the weekly increase in inclination and time in your Training Zone you can adjust things to suit your own circumstances.

Treadmill Week One

For the first week you will set your treadmill to 3%. For most people 3% will not be all that scary. If you just jumped on, set it at 15% and started walking you might feel like you're going to fall off the back of the treadmill. These workouts will be 20:00 to 25:00 long. Try hard to keep your heart rate in the Training Zone for as much of that as you can. With the warm-up and cool-down your workout will be about a half hour. Since your warm-up and cool-down add miles as you achieve them, you can fudge it a bit on the speed and time, and just go for distance. I don't expect you to do math on the fly while walking in the Training Zone on a treadmill set with incline. When you get to about a tenth of a mile to go, drop your speed and walk off that last tenth as your cool-down.

I did the math for you in the example above. Since the weekly mileage goal is less than the weekly mileage required at 3% on the treadmill (3.59 < 5.20) you don't have to make up any excess mileage this week. This will be just a bit stressful perhaps, in trying to hit both a mileage goal and a vertical goal at a fairly fast speed in four rushed hectic sessions.

My recommendation? Four sessions of approximately 1.3 miles, averaging 3.2-3.3 MPH lasting about 30:00 on a treadmill set for 3% inclination. If you cannot make that work no matter what, slow down a bit and just get in some miles and vertical and know that this is the most difficult week of the Adjustment Cycle in that regard.

Treadmill Week Two

For this week, we'll set the treadmill to 6%. This week you should try to extend your working or Training Zone to 30:00 to 35:00. With the warm-up and cool-down that might be right around 40:00 of training.

This week we have a mileage deficit - 3.95 - 2.89 = 1.06. Rather than make that up with a fifth cardio day, I prefer we do it this way, as described here.

Let's do three treadmill sessions at 6% to achieve the vertical goals then the fourth session is just a flat walk on a treadmill or outside with no accounting for vertical.

That works out to three sessions on the treadmill at 6% for .963 miles. The fourth session then is for 1.06 miles at any speed outside or inside, to get in your miles and vertical for the week. If you're shooting for 30:00 of actual training "in the zone" time, that's right around 2.0 MPH which is quite achievable, even at 6% inclination. It should be a "walk in the park" for your non-incline day. That was an intentional pun by the way.

You could do the math and figure out whatever combination of training protocols you think would work best for you, but that's my recommendation.

Treadmill Week Three

This week we're going to increase the inclination to 9%. This could feel somewhat unstable if you're not used to it. Try not to hang on though. We're also shooting for a training time of around 40:00 to 45:00 "in the zone" and with the warm-up and cool-down will be around 50:00.

We have a larger mileage deficit this week. 4.34 miles - 2.14 miles = 2.2 miles that we'll have to make up.

Since we're only looking at 2.14 miles on the treadmill and 40:00 to do it in, we could quite easily do two sessions on the treadmill under incline and two outside or without incline to get in your miles.

This results in two sessions at 9% for 1.07 miles on the treadmill. To do that in 40:00 you'd need to be averaging 1.605 MPH. Still quite achievable. For your two non-incline, or outside walking sessions. you'd need to get in 1.1 miles each, which at the speeds you've been moving at up to now, should only take about a half hour at 2.2 MPH.

Treadmill Week Four

This week we're going to go to 12% inclination now. For many if not most of you this might feel really extreme. You will want to hang on a lot, and even at these quite slow speeds we've been maintaining you might have difficulty staying in your Training Zone. This week try to spend about 50:00 to 55:00 in that zone, and with the warm-up and cool-down you'll be about an hour for a cardio session.

Our deficit will be 3.0 miles this week. If you're strong and can make it work, that could be one single hour long walk in the park. If you want to wander a bit though and not feel pressured for time, split it into two 1.5 mile sessions and at 2.0 MPH that's 45:00, which is pretty close to the 50:00 time target this week.

For the other two sessions, set the treadmill at 12% and go for .89 miles each time. At .97 MPH that's your 55:00 right there. Obviously try to average 1.0 MPH and drop your speed at .88 miles and coast in for a cool-down. If you can do this whole week hands-free, meaning without hanging onto the bars or rails on the treadmill at all, you're ready for what's coming next. If not, we're going ahead with the program, but you'll need to spend some time doing hands-free intervals to wean yourself of the rails.

There are no rails on the trails!

Chart, following, shows all four weeks of the Adjustment Cycle on the treadmill. If you follow the plan as shown you'll make excellent progress. If you need to switch up days, as I've explained before, try hard not to do two back-to-back strength training sessions. I've shown you the math if you'd like to alter the plan to fit your days and times better. This plan assumes four cardio days and two strength training days, and represents a good balance.

Adjustment Cycle Treadmill Goal Chart

Week 1	Week One Training
Monday	Treadmill 3% - 1.30 mi - 30:00 ±
Tuesday	Strength
Wednesday	Treadmill 3% - 1.30 mi - 30:00 ±
Thursday	Strength
Friday	Treadmill 3% - 1.30 mi - 30:00 ±
Saturday	Treadmill 3% - 1.30 mi - 30:00 ±
Week 2	Week Two Training
Monday	Treadmill 6% - .963 mi - 40:00 ±
Tuesday	Strength
Wednesday	Treadmill 6% - .963 mi - 40:00 ±
Thursday	Strength
Friday	1.06 Miles Walking in 40:00 ±
Saturday	Treadmill 6% - .963 mi - 40:00 ±
Week 3	Week Three Training
Monday	Treadmill 9% - 1.07 mi - 50:00 ±
Tuesday	Strength
Wednesday	1.1 Miles Walking in 40:00 ±
Thursday	Strength
Friday	Treadmill 9% - 1.07 mi - 50:00 ±
Saturday	1.1 Miles Walking in 40:00 ±
Week 4	Week Four Training
Monday	Treadmill 12% - .89 mi - 60:00 ±
Tuesday	Strength
Wednesday	1.5 Miles Walking in 50:00 ±
Thursday	Strength
Friday	Treadmill 12% - .89 mi - 60:00 ±
Saturday	1.5 Miles Walking in 50:00 ±

Notes on the Treadmill Program

None of the 14ers a beginner would normally do have a non-stop 4000' ramp at 15%, let alone 40% as on an Incline Treadmill. If you look at the incline treadmill from that perspective, going 5.0 miles at 15% in 4 hours would be nearly 4000' of elevation gain with an average speed of just under 1.3 MPH. We have to train our lower legs to adjust to that angle while not hanging on and keeping our heart rate down in the Training Zone. If you think about it that seems to be not very fast. With training it will seem easier and easier to accomplish. Everyone is in a different place, so relax and don't compare yourself to my goals and charts and targets. It's all adjustment and training and learning how to make it work for yourself in the context of the life you're living. It's quite an adventure and I have sure enjoyed mine. Enjoy yours.

Summit Success

If you're using a Stepmill

Training Week	Target Vertical	Target Miles	SPM Minutes 15	SPM Minutes 20	SPM Minutes 25	SPM Minutes 30
1	824	3.59	82.36	61.77	49.41	41.18
2	915	3.95	91.51	68.63	54.90	45.75
3	1,017	4.34	101.67	76.26	61.00	50.84
4	1,130	4.78	112.97	84.73	67.78	56.49

I would like to repeat here that I prefer that you use the incline setting on a treadmill for this early phase of training. For one thing it's much harder to estimate the fitness levels and progress anyone can make on a Stepmill. I have friends who train on the Stepmill for years and never get much above 30 SPM. My Adjustment Cycle program allows for you to progress to 30 SPM, but you can do a 14er successfully in the time required if you can train long and hard at 25 SPM. It's not easy, but well worth the effort. If you have access to a Stepmill and want to use it for this Adjustment Cycle, here are the directions for the first four weeks.

Note that since this plan is possibly a touch more complicated to assess a goal progression, there will be a separate goal chart for each week of the Adjustment Cycle for the Stepmill program. Since there will be an obvious mileage deficit every week, the program will include time spent walking outside or on a treadmill with the only goal being to get in your miles without any vertical target.

Stepmill Training Basic Instructions

Warm-up: Start with 10 SPM for about 3:00 to 5:00. If your heart rate goes out of the Warm-up Zone, adjust your SPM up or down by 2 SPM at a time to stay within the Warm-up Zone. If your heart rate goes too high, slow down for 0:30 and if it's still high, repeat until it settles into the Warm-up zone. If your heart rate drops below the Warm-up Zone, speed up by 2 SPM every 0:30 until you are in the middle of your Warm-up Zone. Keep your heart rate in that Warm-up Zone as much as possible in the time allotted.

Training: Bump the speed up by 2 SPM. Repeat every 1:30 until your heart rate is in the upper range of the Training Zone. Take a note of what that speed is. If your heart rate goes into the Intensity Zone drop down 2 SPM every 1:30 until you are back into the Training Zone. If your heart rate drops down into the Warm-up Zone then increase your speed by 2 SPM until you are back into the Training Zone. Keep your eyes on your heart rate. Keep this up until you reach about 3:00 to 5:00 from the end of your exercise time, or have completed the set time goal in the Training Zone.

If by some chance your heart rate doesn't get up into the Training Zone, and you end up getting frustrated and bump it up into the 20 SPM + range, then you are most likely sandbagging this and a more advanced trainer. Skip ahead a week or two.

Cool Down: Drop your speed back down to 10 SPM. Hang on. Let your heart rate descend into the Warm-up Zone. If it goes down into the Resting Zone that's fine this week. This will be for 3:00 to 5:00.

Journaling: Get your stats from the console and plug them into my Stepmill Calculator. Keep track of this in your journal. You will need this information to plan out all of the upcoming workouts. Be sure to note the information from my calculator, your max and min SPM, and how you felt. If you thought it was too easy, if you had to use your hands a lot or not at all. It's all important info.

Stepmill Math Example

Let's go with that first week again. You'll need to go for a total of 82.36 minutes at 15 SPM in four sessions.

82.36 total minutes ÷ 4 total sessions = 20.59 minutes per session.

Notice that for the most part I'm using decimal minutes. It makes the charts a lot easier to generate for the book and it makes the math a lot easier to do for you that choose to figure out your own programs.

To convert it back just multiply the decimal portion of the time number by 60 to get the seconds.

.59 minutes x 60 seconds per minute = 35.4 seconds

Close enough to say 36 seconds in my humble opinion.

Summit Success

Stepmill Week One

For the first week you'll set the Stepmill to 15 steps per minute. Some Stepmill models use a Level setting, some allow you to just type in the number you want. Some start with a Level but then when you type in a number it goes that fast. Some you start with a Level then push an up/down or right/left arrow that will change the Level or change the speed. This is not consistent at all. If yours has Levels, start with 1 and go from there to make this work. If you mess around for a minute you'll be able to figure out how to manually adjust your SPM to get the speeds you need to train with your heart rate zones. Sorry I can't be more specific than that. Once you figure out how your Levels compare to Steps Per Minute then you can just hop on and start out with the proper Level to be as close to your targets as possible.

Our target this week is to go 15 SPM or 15 Steps per Minute for 22.59 minutes, as per the math example previously. That's not at all a problem, in general. If you consider as I stated earlier in the book that the Stepmills are generally going to achieve a 99% inclination value, you can assume that the Vertical and Horizontal will be virtually identical. So your Stepmill training for this week will result in a mileage of 824 feet ÷ 5280 feet per mile = .156 miles.

You will have to make up 3.43 miles. You've already done your four full half hour sessions. How do you plan on getting in more training already? If you ask me for my own personal recommendation on it, I would say to just skip it this week. You're getting used to training and adding in 3 more sessions of approximately 1.15 miles would probably break you at this point. Don't risk the upcoming goals over this one. Note for Optional: in case you want some extra training, though I don't recommend it if you're coming in right off the couch and are a total newbie. Save your energy for the Main Training Cycles.

Stepmill Adjustment Cycle Week One Training Chart

Week One	Training	Optional
Monday	Stepmill - 22:35 @ 15 SPM + W/U & C/D = 30:00	Additional 1.15 Miles Walking
Tuesday	Strength	
Wednesday	Stepmill - 22:35 @ 15 SPM + W/U & C/D = 30:00	Additional 1.15 Miles Walking
Thursday	Strength	
Friday	Stepmill - 22:35 @ 15 SPM + W/U & C/D = 30:00	Additional 1.15 Miles Walking
Saturday	Stepmill - 22:35 @ 15 SPM + W/U & C/D = 30:00	

Stepmill Week Two

Now for this week we can make our goals simply enough. At 20 SPM and 30:00 to 35:00 for our training goals we're good to go. I want you to do two sessions of Stepmill training at 20 SPM and 34.3 minutes. With a warm-up and cool-down that's still around the 40:00 target for total training for week two. Remember to try to stay in that Training Zone heart rate for 30:00 to 35:00 if you can.

To make up your Target Miles then you'll have to do 3.77 more miles that week (subtracting out the vertical to horizontal feet from the Stepmill). This should be simple to do with two walks of 1.885 miles. If you want to get them done within the 40:00 time you'll need to walk at about a 2.9 MPH speed. I think for this week if you can't keep that speed up just walk it off to get the miles in that you can in 40:00.

As you get stronger and faster each week it will get a lot easier to get the miles in.

Stepmill Adjustment Cycle Week Two Training Chart

Week Two	Training
Monday	Stepmill - 34:20 @ 20 SPM + W/U & C/D = 40:00
Tuesday	Strength
Wednesday	1.89 Miles Walking in 40:00 ±
Thursday	Strength
Friday	Stepmill - 34:20 @ 20 SPM + W/U & C/D = 40:00
Saturday	1.89 Miles Walking in 40:00 ±

Stepmill Week Three

This week we're going to speed up to 25 SPM. We're going to get in the Training Zone for 40:00 to 45:00 and with warm-up and cool-down, shoot for about 50:00 of training time. Now that causes us to have to jump through a few hoops. The chart calls for our vertical goal to be achieved in only 61 minutes of training on the Stepmill at 25 SPM. No matter how you want to split that up, it's not going to fit into one or two sessions of 50:00 of training.

I think the best way to handle this is to do your warm-up and cool-downs on a treadmill. Do 15:00 on a treadmill with no inclination and 2.0 MPH. Get on the Stepmill for 30:30 set right at 25 SPM with no Stepmill warm-up sequence. Then at the end of your training session get right onto the treadmill again for another 15:00 at 2 MPH. Two of these sessions will get your Vertical Target achieved and 2.0 miles of your Mileage Target achieved.

That leaves you with 2.34 miles to walk off over two more sessions. I didn't subtract the quarter mile of the horizontal Stepmill distance this time. You can go that short of a distance now without quibbling over it. Two sessions of 1.17 miles of walking in the park in 40:00 or so should finish out this week.

I like to be flexible on this. If you're rocking that vertical and want to split it up into four sessions of mixed treadmill and Stepmill training and can figure out how to achieve or overachieve both goals, then go for it.

If for some reason you're not able to progress to 25 SPM or you try it for a few minutes and your heart rate shoots into the Intensity Zone then we'll have to make it work at 20 SPM. If so that's not going to break things. It would be two sessions of 38.13 minutes sandwiched into the treadmill walks. If you bring down your treadmill warm-up and cool-down to 10:00 each at 2.0 mph then you'll end up getting in 1.33 miles in those two sessions. You'll need to make up 3.01 miles then in your two "walk in the park" sessions. That's easy enough to do in 45:00 each at 2.0 MPH.

Stepmill Adjustment Cycle Week Three Training Chart

Week Three	Training Option A 25 SPM	Training Option B 20 SPM
Monday	Treadmill - 15:00 @ 2.0 MPH Stepmill - 30:30 @ 25 SPM Treadmill - 15:00 @ 2.0 MPH	Treadmill - 10:00 @ 2.0 MPH Stepmill - 38:10 @ 20 SPM Treadmill - 10:00 @ 2.0 MPH
Tuesday	Strength	Strength
Wednesday	1.17 Miles Walking in 40:00 ±	1.50 Miles Walking in 45:00 ±
Thursday	Strength	Strength
Friday	Treadmill - 15:00 @ 2.0 MPH Stepmill - 30:30 @ 25 SPM Treadmill - 15:00 @ 2.0 MPH	Treadmill - 10:00 @ 2.0 MPH Stepmill - 38:10 @ 20 SPM Treadmill - 10:00 @ 2.0 MPH
Saturday	1.17 Miles Walking in 40:00 ±	1.50 Miles Walking in 45:00 ±

Option A: 25 SPM

Option B: 20 SPM

Stepmill Week Four

How strong are you feeling? If you're up to it, then let's set the speed to 30 SPM. That might be a lot for some people, and if you're one of them, then let's stay at 25 SPM for this week. I don't want you to get too discouraged. If it's really not working and you've had to stay at 20 SPM for this past two weeks, then we can still make it work. As in other weeks, our target training time has increased to 50:00 to 55:00 and with a warm-up and cool-down we'll be training for about an hour, or 60:00.

First, let's assume you're doing awesome and getting stronger by the day. At 30 SPM you'll need to do one 56.49 minute session. Amazingly, that's about on par with our training time goals this week, so get it done. With the warm-up and cool-down you'll get it done in that hour, easily. If you can go for an hour at 30 SPM. That's really hard for some people. Especially if you've only been training for three weeks and are a total newbie. That leaves you three cardio sessions to get in your 4.78 Mileage Target. Three sessions of 1.6 miles, about 50:00 at 2.0 MPH and you've got it.

You could also do the walking warm-up and cool-down routine a couple times if that helps you get to that speed and eventually the endurance. Over time we're going to increase our endurance, so if you can't get in one straight hour now, then do the whole 15:00 walking at 2.0 SPM warm-up and cool-down sandwiched around 28:15 on the Stepmill at 30 SPM. That leaves us with 2.78 miles to get in with two walking sessions. Just go out for 1.4 miles at 2.0 MPH for about 45:00 and you're done.

If you're still at 20 SPM then do two sessions of 42:22 on the Stepmill at 20 SPM and try to get in 8:00 each of warm-up and cool-down on the treadmill at 2.0 MPH. You'll end up getting in 1.06 miles that way, and will have 3.72 miles to achieve your goal. Two sessions outside walking in the park of 1.856 miles at 2.0 MPH for 56:00 and you've got your goals met.

If you're at 25 SPM, that's two sessions of 34:00 on the Stepmill surrounded by a warm-up and cool-down of 13:00 at 2.0 MPH on the treadmill. You'll get in 1.73 miles. Add in two sessions of walking at 2.0 MPH for 1.53 miles, taking about 46:00.

That's the simplest way I know to do this type of planning. If it doesn't make sense just do what I put down for your goals. If it makes sense and you want to play with it, making your own custom combinations of days and times and miles then certainly, go ahead and make it work for you.

The following chart shows all four options discussed here. Try to make the best of it, and if there is any way you can accomplish Option A, then by all means, get it done and feel like you have achieved something great.

Option A: Single 30 SPM training session

Option B: 30 SPM training sessions with walking warm-up/cool-down

Option C: 20 SPM training sessions with walking warm-up/cool-down

Option D: 25 SPM training sessions with walking warm-up/cool-down

Stepmill Adjustment Cycle Week Four Training Chart

Week Four	Training Option A	Training Option B
Monday	1.60 Miles Walking in 50:00 ±	Treadmill - 15:00 @ 2.0 MPH Stepmill - 28:15 @ 30 SPM Treadmill - 15:00 @ 2.0 MPH
Tuesday	Strength	Strength
Wednesday	1.60 Miles Walking in 50:00 ±	1.40 Miles Walking in 45:00 ±
Thursday	Strength	Strength
Friday	Stepmill - 56:30 @ 30 SPM + W/U & C/D = 65:00	Treadmill - 15:00 @ 2.0 MPH Stepmill - 28:15 @ 30 SPM Treadmill - 15:00 @ 2.0 MPH
Saturday	1.60 Miles Walking in 50:00 ±	1.40 Miles Walking in 45:00 ±
Week Four	Training Option C	Training Option D
Monday	Treadmill - 8:00 @ 2.0 MPH Stepmill - 42:22 @ 20 SPM Treadmill - 8:00 @ 2.0 MPH	Treadmill - 13:00 @ 2.0 MPH Stepmill - 34:00 @ 25 SPM Treadmill - 13:00 @ 2.0 MPH
Tuesday	Strength	Strength
Wednesday	1.86 Miles Walking in 56:00 ±	1.53 Miles Walking in 46:00 ±
Thursday	Strength	Strength
Friday	Treadmill - 8:00 @ 2.0 MPH Stepmill - 42:22 @ 20 SPM Treadmill - 8:00 @ 2.0 MPH	Treadmill - 13:00 @ 2.0 MPH Stepmill - 34:00 @ 25 SPM Treadmill - 13:00 @ 2.0 MPH
Saturday	1.86 Miles Walking in 56:00 ±	1.53 Miles Walking in 46:00 ±

Notes on the Stepmill Program

After reading this you might feel like the Stepmill program is a bit more intense than the treadmill program. That's true. The Stepmill is set at a nearly 45 degree angle. That's a 100% incline (meaning that over a 100' distance you have a 100' rise in elevation) which is steeper than you can get on most commercially available treadmills. By default it's already way more intense than a treadmill. I'm starting out with rather conservative Step per Minute settings, and in your own workouts you might only get 1-4 SPM above my initial settings as outlined here. You might have to spend some time at half of my initial settings. That's fine. The beauty of this program is that it's totally built around your own limitations and abilities.

With the ultimate goal of doing a 14er, not one of the mountains here has a continuous non-stop 3500' ramp at 100% incline. If you were able to stay on a Stepmill for 4 hours at 25 SPM you'd climb 4000' of vertical. When all is said and done, that alone is a worthy target and would accomplish our goal of training for our 14er. If you can't go more than 16 SPM without your heart rate going into the Intensity Zone, that's great for now. We have 12 weeks yet to get that last 9 SPM while staying in the Training Zone.

If you're using a Box or Stairs

Training Week	Target Vertical	Target Miles	Steps at 6"	Steps at 9"	Steps at 12"
1	824	3.59	1647	1098	824
2	915	3.95	1830	1220	915
3	1,017	4.34	2033	1356	1017
4	1,130	4.78	2259	1506	1130

So long as you strive to get in your miles some other way, you can use a Box or Stairs to train for your mountain. It's great in a few ways, but primarily it's one of the best ways to get in some overcompensation training for the descent using the eccentric, or negative motion of stepping down steeply as much as you are ascending.

If you're using a box, you get the negative in on every step sequence. If you're using the stairs you get the negative in when you hit the top of your flights of stairs and go back to the bottom. That depends on how many flights you have access to. I have access to an apartment building with three floors, so that's only two flights with four landings.

If you don't have access to an official Plyo or Jump Box (found at many gyms) you can make do with just about any type of stable surface so long as you measure it to be the right height for your training goals. It also has to be extremely stable. I mention stable a lot because you might not consider the effects of inertia and gravity when stepping up onto what you would normally consider to be a stable surface. In general you trust your kitchen chairs to keep you from falling to the floor. Just stand on a corner with your toes and toss your body weight up into the air to watch it flip and spin under you. Wait. That was merely an example. Don't really do it. Please. So be very careful to make sure that your "box" will be stable from various directions and with various forces. In the illustrations I've done just that.

In the following illustrations 1) I'm using a stump by the river here in Colorado that is 9" on the side I'm stepping on. The opposite side is 6" so could easily be used for a previous week or lesser goal. 2) I'm showing the same 9" stump used with my trekking poles for balance and minimal assistance. 3, 4) I'm showing a few different angles using an 18" park bench as a box for stepping. Because that's too high to reach the poles in the upper position I'm setting the poles on the bench for this training example. I think 18" is too high for most people, and even for very strong people it would be difficult to maintain a 30 steps per minute pace for any real length of time. It's also quite a bit more dangerous and the consequences of a minor slip are not worth the risk.

Summit Success

Training for Hiking, Mountaineering, and Peak Bagging – by Charles Miske

Summit Success

Training for Hiking, Mountaineering, and Peak Bagging – by Charles Miske

Summit Success

Stairs are a little bit simpler than boxes in that you have a course laid out before you and you don't have to count 2000 steps in a workout. You can count landings or bottom to top laps. You also don't have to worry about always using the same foot over and over without thinking about it at all. That's quite common on a box.

In the following illustrations I'll show what it looks like, first inside. As though you've never gone up and down stairs? Notice that on the downward side I'm lightly gripping the rail for balance. I want you to do that too. Going down is the most dangerous part of stairs and I don't want you to fall now. It would mess up the next 16 weeks if nothing else.

In the next illustration I'm outside on some good solid timber stairs. These are the ones I used for my training video as mentioned as an extra available on my website. Notice in both photos that I'm keeping my arms poised for balance and control.

Training for Hiking, Mountaineering, and Peak Bagging – by Charles Miske

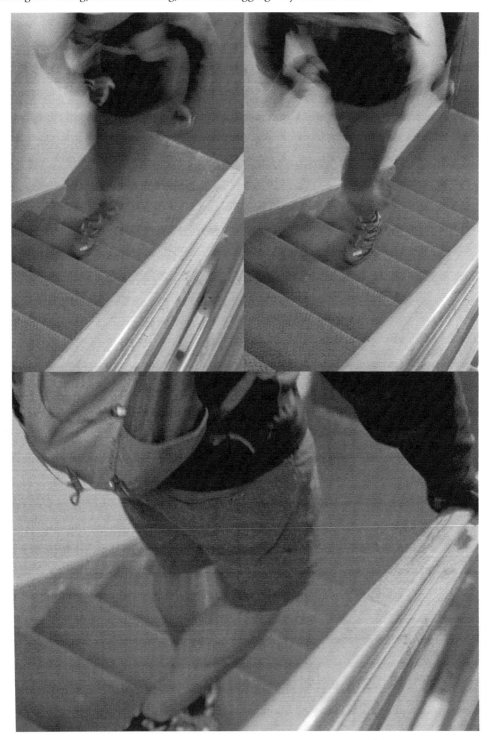

Summit Success

Stairs Math Example

I will repeat all of this once more in the Main Training section of the book, just to make sure you really understand it, so when you get there, and you do understand it, then by all means skim or skip it.

Let's do a quick example to show how to calculate your box stepping session goals, again, from Week One. Assume we measured our stairs in our apartment building and they are 9" vertical rise, with 11 steps per landing. I'm trying to make this simple, as you'll see in the math below:

Week One Example using 9" Stairs with Landings:

1098 steps ÷ 11 steps per landing = 100 landings

100 landings ÷ 4 training sessions = 25 landings per training session

Since it's the first week, you're going to want to do a minute per landing to total your 25:00 training time. For myself I do not do a formal warm-up and cool-down when I'm doing stairs. I just go a bit slower until my knees feel good and then the last few times I go up and down I go a bit slower to cool down. Note that I said down. A minute per landing might seem really slow to you. Since odds are your apartment building does not have 25 consecutive landings, you will have to descend every so many landings. Descending does not count as ascending and is not part of your vertical goal achievement. You will have to hit your landings and return to the start and do laps of your stairways until you have achieved your daily training goal. I don't want you hopping from landing to landing like a teenager and getting hurt or stumbling down and breaking something important. Like you. So when you add up your times, be sure to keep in mind it has to include your descent as well.

Week One Example using 9" Stairs without Landings:

1098 steps ÷ 2 training sessions = 549 steps per training session

549 steps ÷ 20 steps per minute = 27.45 minutes

549 steps ÷ 40 steps from bottom to top = 13.75 trips up and down

Without landings on your staircase, or if they're unevenly distributed (as in some landings are 8 steps apart and some are 9) you'll need to count total steps then. In this example there are 40 steps from the ground floor to the top floor. Since in the upcoming training programs I have no idea how many steps you have available for training, I'll give the total count and expect you to figure out how many trips up and down you'll need to achieve your goal.

Box Stepping Math Example

If you're going to use a box, you will get your eccentric, or downhill training, on every step. You count a step as every time your shoulders come up over the box with your legs and hips "straightened" but don't exaggerate the motion, please. One advantage to this is that you can set a metronome app with an intended pace that is more difficult to achieve on stairs. Stairs have landings, often with turns, that prevent adhering strictly to the ticking of a metronome.

Usually, you face the box, step up with one foot, bring the other foot up beside it and straighten. You return to the beginning by reversing the motion and then repeat. Be very careful that you don't bang your legs on the edges of the box. If you don't have an official box you could possibly get away with using a stair, a park bench, a picnic table. Just make sure it's going to hold your weight under dynamic force. You could be applying 300 pounds or more of multi-directional pressure in the middle of a step. You do not want to be flipping a picnic table over on yourself. Just saying.

The metronome app I've experimented with allows me to set a pace, say 20 beats per minute, then give an alternate alert tone every 10 or 15 beats, or steps as I'm using it. The setting for that is *Beats-per-Bar*. I can also set it to alert me with another tone for the in-between steps called *Clicks-per-Beat*. UP, up, down, down, UP, up, down, down, UP, up, down, down….

If I set a goal to take 250 steps that day, I can just listen for the big alert tone 25 times at 10 Beats per Bar. Unless your heart rate is out of this world, you can manage to keep that level of awareness for that amount of time.

Week One Example Using 6" Box:

1647 steps ÷ 4 training sessions = 412 steps per training session

412 steps ÷ 20 steps per minute = 20.6 minutes

412 steps ÷ 15 step sets = 27.5 sets

For training over your target, if you're using a metronome as I would be, then you just have to listen to the big beat 28 times and you're done. Just keep your feet moving to the beat and it'll be a fantastic workout. If you want more info on my metronome app settings, in the above example it would be set for:

- 20 Beats per Minute
- 15 Beats per Measure
- 4 Clicks per Beat

You can use anything you want that makes it work for you. Metronome, stopwatch, phone apps, music with the right beats. Make it happen and you can get to the top.

Stairs Week One

Stairs are a lot more cut and dried than boxes, simply because a stair tread is a set height and while you could wander around measuring stairs till you find sets of 6" or 12" stairs, I'm going to assume you have a fairly average set of 9" stairs to deal with. Even if it is 8" that's within about 11% in the big scheme of things, so just add in 11% more steps and you have it. I already went through the math previously. If you want to redo my math with the 8" stair, if that's what you have, then by all means, go ahead.

Since I don't know anything about your landings, it's better if I just do the math for this one without landings and just go for the steps per session. If you're training at a stadium you might have small landings every 30 steps or so. It's mostly a tool for counting steps without having to think a lot. If you know you have to do 400 steps that's tougher to count than if you know you have 40 landings. You should be able to just hold up fingers from hand to hand to count to 40. If you know you have 40 steps from the bottom to the top, then just do 10 times to the top and back. You can figure it out.

Our goal this week then is two training sessions of 27:30 in which you get in 549 steps. If you go slower for a couple minutes at the beginning and end for a warm-up and cool-down you'll be about 30:00 on the stairs twice. As in the Stepmill protocols, we're not going to really consider the mileage from the stairs at all. You'll then have to do two training sessions of walking on the treadmill our outdoors without any appreciable vertical gain of about 1.8 miles each. It would be very difficult to get in 1.8 miles in only 30:00 for most people trying to keep their heart rate down in their Training Zone, but for just this week, let's go to about 45:00 to 60:00 and it should be achievable for most everyone. Just go as fast as your heart rate allows.

Stairs Week Two

This week we're going to get in 1220 total steps and 3.95 miles while going for 40:00 total per training session including warm-up and cool-down.

That works out to two sessions of 610 steps in 30:30 (at 20 SPM average) and with a little warm-up and cool-down, easily achievable in 40:00 total. The other two sessions are walking 1.98 miles in about 50:00 at a little faster than 2.0 MPH. If you can go 3.0 MPH on your walking course or treadmill then you could get it done in 40:00 without too much difficulty.

Stairs Week Three

For this week we're going to climb 1356 steps and walk 4.34 miles for about 50:00 total training time in each session. We'll do two stair climbing sessions of 678 steps in 34:00 (at 20 SPM average), and we get a very mellow warm-up and cool-down to get in our 50:00 total training time. If you'd rather mix things up and do your warm-up and cool-down by walking and subtract it from the walking totals, that's fine.

For our two walking sessions we'll be doing 2.17 miles in about 50:00 which is 2.6 MPH. If you can't go that fast, then take some miles for your warm-up and cool-down on stairs days, or go a bit longer to make it work.

Stairs Week Four

This is our last week in the Adjustment Cycle. For some of the other training equipment protocols it's building up to a pretty fast and difficult workout. For the stairs though, 9" is 9" any way you look at it. Next week you get the backpack, so if you're a little bored and wanting to make it more exciting remember that you chose stairs, and that you'll start adding in weight next week.

We're going to hit 1506 steps and 4.78 miles this week. That's 753 steps in 37:40 and a quite reasonable warm-up and cool-down to equal 60:00. Again, you can borrow miles from the mileage goal and walk before and/or after your stairs session. For walking we'll do 2.39 miles in 60:00 which is 2.4 MPH and quite achievable, especially after a few weeks getting into the groove.

Adjustment Cycle Stairs Goal Chart

Weekdays	Week One Training
Monday	Stairs 549 Steps in 27:30 + w/u, c/d = 30:00
Tuesday	Strength
Wednesday	1.8 Miles Walking in 50:00 ±
Thursday	Strength
Friday	Stairs 549 Steps in 27:30 + w/u, c/d = 30:00
Saturday	1.8 Miles Walking in 50:00 ±
Weekdays	Week Two Training
Monday	Stairs 610 Steps in 30:30 + w/u, c/d = 40:00
Tuesday	Strength
Wednesday	1.98 Miles Walking in 50:00 ±
Thursday	Strength
Friday	Stairs 610 Steps in 30:30 + w/u, c/d = 40:00
Saturday	1.98 Miles Walking in 50:00 ±
Weekdays	Week Three Training
Monday	Stairs 678 Steps in 34:00 + w/u, c/d = 50:00
Tuesday	Strength
Wednesday	2.17 Miles Walking in 50:00 ±
Thursday	Strength
Friday	Stairs 678 Steps in 34:00 + w/u, c/d = 50:00
Saturday	2.17 Miles Walking in 50:00 ±
Weekdays	Week Four Training
Monday	Stairs 753 Steps in 37:40 + w/u, c/d = 60:00
Tuesday	Strength
Wednesday	2.39 Miles Walking in 60:00 ±
Thursday	Strength
Friday	Stairs 753 Steps in 37:40 + w/u, c/d = 60:00
Saturday	2.39 Miles Walking in 60:00 ±

Box Week One

For training on the box, since you're going up and down a lot on each step, you might be happier on a 6" box until you get used to it. I also recommend a conservative 20 SPM (Steps per Minute) pace. If you are in really good shape you might be able to get away with a 9" box if you have access to one. Since there are a variety of things you can step on if you dig around for a few minutes, it's a lot easier to do more fine adjustments. You can find 6" concrete curbs quite easily. You can find some 9" curbs or timber flower bed surrounds. It's all up to you.

If you're using a 6" step, which I think a lot of total beginners right off the couch might opt for, that's 1647 steps. That's a lot. If you do box stepping for all four sessions this week that's 412 steps each session. At 20 SPM that's 20:40, and fills up a whole training session so that with warm-up and cool-down we're at about 30:00. If you recall in previous descriptions (if you didn't skim over them) this first week can be tough for getting in your mileage while keeping training sessions less than thirty minutes. If that's the case, then go ahead. We'll be doing better next week for sure.

If you're strong and want to start with the 9" step, then it's the same as the stairs week one in the last section. You get two training sessions of 27:30 in which you get in 549 steps. If you go slower for a couple minutes at the beginning and end for a warm-up and cool-down you'll be about 30:00 on the stairs twice. Then you would have two sessions available for walking 1.8 miles each. As I mentioned previously, it would be very difficult to get in 1.8 miles in only 30:00 for most people trying to keep their heart rate down in their Training Zone, but for just this week, let's go to about 45:00 to 60:00 and it should be achievable for most everyone. Remember though to go as fast as your heart rate allows while not getting into the Intensity Zone.

Box Adjustment Cycle Week One Training Chart

Weekdays	Week One Training 6"	Week One Training 9"
Monday	6" box - 412 Steps in 20:40 + w/u, c/d = 30:00	9" box - 549 Steps in 27:30 + w/u, c/d = 30:00
Tuesday	Strength	Strength
Wednesday	6" box - 412 Steps in 20:40 + w/u, c/d = 30:00	1.8 Miles Walking in 50:00 ±
Thursday	Strength	Strength
Friday	6" box - 412 Steps in 20:40 + w/u, c/d = 30:00	9" box - 549 Steps in 27:30 + w/u, c/d = 30:00
Saturday	6" box - 412 Steps in 20:40 + w/u, c/d = 30:00	1.8 Miles Walking in 50:00 ±

First training column is for a 6" box and includes no walking or mileage achievements.

Second training column is for a 9" box and includes walking cardio sessions to get in your mileage goals.

Box Week Two

This week we'll also do a 6" and 9" option. For 6" our goal is 1830 steps over 3 training sessions of 610 steps in 30:30 (at 20 SPM average). That easily fits into the 40:00 target with warm-up and cool-down of about 4:45 each. We are left with one session of walking available, and we'll do half of the miles in the goal in one session of 1.98 miles in about 50:00 at a bit faster than 2.0 MPH. We're getting there steady and slow.

For the 9" goal, we're again following the lead from our 9" stairs second week training sessions. That's 1220 total steps in two sessions of 610 steps in 30:30 (at 20 SPM average) and with a little warm-up and cool-down, easily achievable in 40:00 total. If you're at all curious why these two sessions listed here are similar, it's because $6/9 = 2/3$. So 3 sessions at 6" should be equal to 2 sessions at 9" and makes this math easy to figure out.

The other two sessions in the 9" training protocol this week are walking 1.98 miles in about 50:00 at a little faster than 2.0 MPH. If you can go 3.0 MPH on your walking course or treadmill then you could get it done in 40:00 without too much difficulty.

Training for Hiking, Mountaineering, and Peak Bagging – by Charles Miske

Box Adjustment Cycle Week Two Training Chart

Weekdays	Week Two Training 6"	Week Two Training 9"
Monday	6" box - 610 Steps in 30:30 + w/u, c/d = 40:00	9" box - 610 Steps in 30:30 + w/u, c/d = 40:00
Tuesday	Strength	Strength
Wednesday	6" box - 610 Steps in 30:30 + w/u, c/d = 40:00	1.8 Miles Walking in 50:00 ±
Thursday	Strength	Strength
Friday	1.8 Miles Walking in 50:00 ±	9" box - 610 Steps in 30:30 + w/u, c/d = 40:00
Saturday	6" box - 610 Steps in 30:30 + w/u, c/d = 40:00	1.8 Miles Walking in 50:00 ±

Training options for 6" and 9" box. If you had difficulty last week with the 6" box, stick with it for this week, but next week we need to graduate to the 9" box.

Summit Success

Box Week Three

This week we get onto the 9" and 12" boxes. For the 9" box, as in the stairs week three previously discussed, we're going to climb 1356 steps and walk 4.34 miles for about 50:00 total training time in each session. We'll do two stair climbing sessions of 678 steps in 34:00 (at 20 SPM average), and we get a very mellow warm-up and cool-down to get in our 50:00 total training time. If you'd rather mix things up and do your warm-up and cool-down by walking and subtract it from the walking totals, that's fine.

For our two walking sessions we'll be doing 2.17 miles in about 50:00 which is 2.6 MPH. If you can't go that fast, then take some miles for your warm-up and cool-down on stairs days, or go a bit longer to make it work.

For the 12" box, we'll need to do 1017 steps. We could do it in one 51:00 training session, but that's a huge jump from last week, in both training time and height of step. It's better than to go for the walking warm-up/cool-down protocol we explored earlier.

That gives us two sessions of 25:30 in which we do 509 steps (at 20 SPM average). Add in 10:00 of walking both before and after at a 2.0 MPH average for a total of 1.33 miles between the two sessions, and that leaves us with 3.0 miles to make up in two walking sessions of 1.5 miles in 45:00 at 2.0 MPH or a little shorter if you're faster.

Box Adjustment Cycle Week Three Training Chart

Weekdays	Week Three Training 9"	Week Three Training 12"
Monday	9" box - 678 Steps in 34:00 + w/u, c/d = 50:00	Walking - 10:00 @ 2.0 MPH 12" box - 509 Steps in 25:30 Walking - 10:00 @ 2.0 MPH
Tuesday	Strength	Strength
Wednesday	2.17 Miles Walking in 50:00 ±	1.5 Miles Walking in 45:00 ±
Thursday	Strength	Strength
Friday	9" box - 678 Steps in 34:00 + w/u, c/d = 50:00	Walking - 10:00 @ 2.0 MPH 12" box - 509 Steps in 25:30 Walking - 10:00 @ 2.0 MPH
Saturday	2.17 Miles Walking in 50:00 ±	1.5 Miles Walking in 45:00 ±

Options shown for 9" and 12" box. If you did great with the 9" box last week then try the 12" if you want to make progress. Otherwise do the 9" box, and next week we'll see if you can bump up to the 12" box.

Box Week Four

This is the last week of the Adjustment Cycle. If you're stuck at 9" or haven't even done the 9" don't fret. But don't slack either. Next week is the start of your Main Training Cycle, so we're going to go for the 12" box then if not before.

For the 9" box, like in the stairs training protocol, we're going to hit 1506 steps and 4.78 miles this week. That's 753 steps in 37:40. We're going to sandwich that in between two warm-up and cool-down blocks of 10:00 each at 2.0 MPH to get us up to the 60:00 time goal for training sessions this week. We'll take that 1.33 miles off the 4.78 so we have to get in two 1.75 mile walking cardio sessions to finish off the week.

If we're going for the 12" box, then we're going to climb 1130 steps. That's two sessions of 565 steps in 28:15 (at 20 SPM average). We'll go ahead and do the walking before and after for the warm-up and cool-down at 15:00 each to get up to the 60:00 mark and an additional 2.0 miles of walking in. That leaves us with 2.78 miles of walking to get in with two session of 1.4 miles in about 45:00 at a 2.0 MPH average.

Box Adjustment Cycle Week Four Training Chart

Weekdays	Week Three Training 9"	Week Three Training 12"
Monday	Walking - 10:00 @ 2.0 MPH 9" box - 753 Steps in 37:40 Walking - 10:00 @ 2.0 MPH	Walking - 15:00 @ 2.0 MPH 12" box - 565 Steps in 28:15 Walking - 15:00 @ 2.0 MPH
Tuesday	Strength	Strength
Wednesday	1.75 Miles Walking in 50:00 ±	1.4 Miles Walking in 45:00 ±
Thursday	Strength	Strength
Friday	Walking - 10:00 @ 2.0 MPH 9" box - 753 Steps in 37:40 Walking - 10:00 @ 2.0 MPH	Walking - 15:00 @ 2.0 MPH 12" box - 565 Steps in 28:15 Walking - 15:00 @ 2.0 MPH
Saturday	1.75 Miles Walking in 50:00 ±	1.4 Miles Walking in 45:00 ±

This week we're doing a lot more walking as part of the warm-up and cool-down for both the 9" and 12" box options. If you can't do the 12" this week, be prepared to do it next week for certain.

Box and Stairs Considerations Examined

Most of all for these, I want you to consider safety much more than on the treadmills and Stepmills. Hundreds of engineering hours were put into the machinery to help protect you from yourself. The same can't be said of stairs and boxes. The commercial Plyo Boxes were designed to have a reasonable margin of safety, though I imagine you could YouTube it and find a slew of Plyo Box Fails to enjoy and possibly learn from.

That being said, I've gone over it time after time here in this book. I want you to be careful and don't get hurt and don't get dead. I missed stepping down once from a 24" Plyo Box and ended up falling through the rails of a nearby treadmill. Thankfully it wasn't being used at the time and I got a great cut on my forearm from trying to grab the rail on the way past.

So be warned. It's really dangerous. Be very careful at all times and try to stay alert and aware. It's especially important if you're doing this on anything that isn't meant to be used this way. I've mentioned park benches, picnic tables, curbs and planter boxes. I'm only pointing those out as suggestions for where to start looking. Use common sense and don't use anything that is slippery or unstable or has the potential for dire consequences if you miss a step or slip off.

If you are Running or Walking Outside

If you are going to be training outside, or at least not on machinery, then I'd like you to try your best to emulate either program. First let's explore the Treadmill Program. Finding an outdoor training path with similar average stats might be difficult or not, depending on where you live. You can find Facebook, Google, Yahoo, Strava or other training Groups and Boards where you can ask questions and research your area. If you can find a steep hill and lap it, average your distance and time to emulate the training protocols as best you can.

If you are planning on being outside a lot on relatively flat surfaces, then please back up a step and see if you can do the Box Stepping protocol above on a park bench or other strong stable durable surface. Just don't slip off of surfaces that have a lot less friction than you expect, like epoxy coated benches, truck bumpers, etc.

Here's the chart with the most basic information, if you're going to try to make it work using steep grades. You'll have to do your own math, sorry, since I have no idea which of several hundreds of thousands of trails or roads you'll be on. If you're motivated, the answer is in the math.

Training Week	Target Vertical	Target Miles
1	824	3.59
2	915	3.95
3	1,017	4.34
4	1,130	4.78

Remember, during the Adjustment Cycle we're learning how to make it all work and how we're going to train smart and create our own individual goals and targets for training.

4 Week Adjustment Cycle Calendar

Sunday	Monday	Tuesday	Wednesday	Thursday	Friday	Saturday
Rest Day Week One	Cardio: 20:00	Strength: GPP Workout	Cardio: 20:00	Strength: GPP Workout	Cardio: 20:00	Cardio: 20:00
Rest Day Week Two	Cardio: 30:00	Strength: GPP Workout	Cardio: 30:00	Strength: GPP Workout	Cardio: 30:00	Cardio: 30:00
Rest Day Week Three	Cardio: 40:00	Strength: GPP Workout	Cardio: 40:00	Strength: GPP Workout	Cardio: 40:00	Cardio: 40:00
Rest Day Week Four	Cardio: 50:00	Strength: GPP Workout	Cardio: 50:00	Strength: GPP Workout	Cardio: 50:00	Cardio: 50:00
Begin - Main Training Cycle						

This training cycle calendar is a suggestion for how to get in the workouts outlined here for the first training cycle, the 4 Week Adjustment Cycle. It's up to you how to make it work in your own training schedule. In this example I've kept Sunday open as your regular rest day. You must take a rest day each week. It's better if it's always the same day each week. I myself prefer to do my Strength Training days earlier in the week and have two consecutive Cardio Training days near the end of the week. If you need to slide things around a bit, here are a couple suggestions.

- Don't have more than two consecutive Cardio Training Days.
- Don't do two consecutive Strength Training Days.

Strength Training for the First Four Weeks

Right now you're adjusting to the cardio workouts and learning how your body reacts and what levels and speeds and setting you need for your current fitness levels. On top of that we'll also be doing the same thing with strength training. This is the period in which you figure out where you stand in regards to your strength. If you already strength train regularly, then some of these exercises might seem a bit basic to you.

In general I'm a bit old-school that way. I much prefer the classics for strength workouts. If you're already weight training then please read the exercises I've selected as most important to a beginning trainer and see how they compare to what you're doing. If you can adjust your own training program a bit to accommodate doing these, or a variation on these, please do so. If you're limited on time for training, then you should focus less on isolation exercises for the "vanity muscles" like biceps, which have little to do with hiking.

Your upper body needs to be strong enough to carry your backpack, swing your trekking poles, and assist with balance in the event you stumble. The upper body muscles also come into play on the descent when you reach down with your trekking poles to stay in balance or to take some of the weight off your legs. Your arms will only be assisting a little bit here and there, without any maximal effort movements. You will not have to do any full body weight pull-ups to do a 14er by the normal routes.

Your lower body will need to carry your own weight, plus the weight of your backpack with food, water and extra clothing in it. Add in a little for whatever shoes or boots you're wearing. You might have to step up onto the occasional boulder or rock step, but your arms will be assisting you with your trekking poles, or holding onto the edge of the rock. You should not have to do any one-legged full body weight movements.

Your core is the connection between your upper and lower body. Your strength and endurance originate in your core. That's the center of your motion and control. Your core needs to be strong so that when you reach down with a trekking pole to step down from a boulder, you can control the amount of pressure so that the tip of your pole doesn't pop out of the gravel and dirt, yet your step down is centered and slow enough that you can change direction as needed so that you won't roll your ankle in the gravel. It all just comes naturally, you don't have to think too hard about how that works. But you do need to be strong enough.

With all that in mind I have planned your strength workouts to include some upper body work, some lower body work, and some core work. You'll notice it's a little heavy on lower body, but that's because we'll need a lot of lower body strength endurance to succeed with our mountain hike at the end of the program. Especially in the early stages, while we're first learning how to train, I prefer light duty workouts using body weight where possible. I also like the large rubber bands, but you can use the cables on towers or functional trainers as well if that's what you have access to. If you have weights, dumbbells kettle bells or barbells or can train at a gym, I can show you how to do that too.

If you have a heart rate monitor that you can use for Strength Training, then by all means go ahead. Whether it is a watch or a phone app, you can make it work. I think it would be great if you can keep it in the Warm-up Zone for your entire Strength Training session. If you can keep it in the Training Zone that's actually quite an achievement.

I propose that you spend about 5:00 warming up, then about 5:00 of Light Stretching, 5:00 of Core Work, then about 25:00 to 30:00 of Strength Training. This adds up to about 45:00 of training time. That's pretty easy for most people to squeeze into their routines without a great deal of adjustment. The Training Calendar calls for two Strength Training sessions each week. The program for now is, again, in bullet points:

- 5:00 - Warm-Up
- 5:00 - Light Stretching
- 5:00 - Core Training
- 30:00 - Strength Training

For each of the Strength Training Exercises I want you to do 3 sets of 10. Example:

Squats 10 @ BW x 3

That's Squats, 10 reps at Body Weight x 3 sets, if you recall from the Journaling Chapter. I want you to do each set within a one minute chunk of time. If you do a 2 second up, 2 second down cadence, that would be about 40 seconds for a set, with 20 seconds of rest between each set. That's actually quite reasonable. Even if you add in a few seconds here and there you'll end up only adding about 5:00 to your total workout. If you crash and burn and have to rest for a few minutes here and there the whole thing should still come in under an hour.

If you crash and burn during the Adjustment Cycle it means you're pushing too hard.

I've created a protocol with 8 different Strength Training Exercises for this program. As I've explained above, we're going to do a bit more leg work, and the upper body work is primarily to support our packs and poles and alleviate fatigue. This is a classic GPP or "General Physical Preparation" Workout Protocol. Every week has two Strength Training sessions, with a day or two of Cardio between them during the Adjustment Cycle.

Adjustment Cycle Strength Training Considerations

Right now your goal isn't to become a bodybuilder or powerlifter. You're trying to increase your strength endurance foundation to achieve your goal of training to hike and climb a mountain. You shouldn't fail during any of these sets, especially during your Adjustment Cycle.

If you're in set number one and can't do your 5th rep you are using way too much resistance. If you're doing Chin-ups that might not be unexpected. If you get to set number 3 and can't get rep number 9 in, just don't stress and see if in the next workout you can.

Right now you're trying to figure this out, especially if you are coming in off the couch and have never done these exercises before. If you have done them before and are used to doing a different set and rep pattern, or are used to going to failure, you might have to adjust your weights down some to prevent failure.

You'll have a lot of waste products in your body from your cardio training, so you don't want to make recovery any harder by failing at strength training. Failing affects your hormones and other body chemistry in ways that are great for building muscle if you know how to manage your recovery. Since our primary goal is not to get huge, we'll worry about recovering from our cardio training.

Right now focus on your strength training as support for your cardio training, not as your primary goal. When your mountain is climbed you can switch to full-on bodybuilder or powerlifter mode. That being said, I also need to mention artificial and chemical supplements designed to promote faster recovery. Please do not start taking anything new. For one thing, many people respond differently to them, and for another, a lot of it is just marketing. Don't get hooked into some supplement that will promise the world to make a sale.

Good basic electrolytes and salts, with lots of pure plain cold water in addition to a health-promoting diet without fads and gimmicks will go a long way toward helping your body recover naturally. Try that for a while, like 20 weeks, and see how it works for you.

Strength Training

Now for the meat of the program, the Strength Training Exercises. Remember, we're doing 24 total sets of 10 reps. That is 3 sets of 10 for each of 8 exercises. I would like each set to last about a minute including the reps and rest. Just keep moving and you'll have a great workout with a good pump. If you're opting to do the Unilateral Variation of some of the exercises, for the most effective training and efficient use of time, do one side, then the other, then rest.

I want you to log everything, so make sure you count your sets and reps and weights and be honest. You'll want to try to make progress but you also don't want to burn out and miss working out. You especially don't want to miss out on a cardio training session. It's a fine line to walk, so I'd rather you be cautious with making progress in your strength training.

First we're going to work larger muscle groups with compound movements, then narrow down at the end with some isolation movements. The first ones are the most important, but that doesn't mean you can slack off on the last ones. They just take less energy, but perhaps more mental focus since you might find yourself quite tired by the time you're done. I want you to do these in the order presented if possible, but please, if you're in a commercial or shared gym environment skip around if needed to keep moving with little rest.

For clothing you can wear the same running shorts and top as in the Cardio Training sessions, but I prefer a pair of sweat pants and a cotton shirt for Strength Training. It's just personal preference. I don't think thick soled shoes are appropriate for Strength Training, but that's just me. You might prefer it. Hiking boots are great though. That being said I usually wear very thin running shoes for my own training. I can't recommend that for everyone though.

Begin with a good warm-up and end with a good cool-down. The idea isn't to get in another cardio workout, but just to get the blood flowing and the joints loose. Then do about a half hour of strength training between them, including a decent core workout.

Here are the details.

Warm-Up

First begin with about five to ten minutes, 5:00-10:00 of something that will warm up your joints and get the blood flowing. Try to get in the whole body, but if it's only the legs that's fine, since we won't be using big weights for our upper body. Most of us anyway.

You can use an Elliptical Machine, a Rowing Machine, do Walking Lunges or Box Stepping for that time. I prefer that you not use a Stepmill or Treadmill, simply because that's what you're doing for the rest of the week, and I want your body to have a break from that routine at least these two days and one rest day each week. Later in the program we'll change that, but for now see if you can use one of these alternatives.

My own personal preference is almost always for the Elliptical, but I do use a Rowing Machine on a fairly regular basis. Now and then I'll do a cycle of Box Stepping, which I particularly like for training the Eccentric, or Negative, or Stepping Down portion of the movement. If you have access to a gym, do the Rowing Machine or Elliptical. If not, then the Lunges and Box Stepping will be effective. If over time you notice that you are having trouble walking downhill then focus more on the Lunges and Box Stepping, both of which have Eccentric Movement involved.

Some people need more warm-up time than others. That's okay. Take what time you need. Some days I get enough warm-up from my first set of weights. Other days I need a good 10:00 on the Elliptical to loosen up my joints. You'll learn over time what works best for you. Start with 5:00 and adjust up from there. Right now I want you to take at least the 5:00, unless you're an advanced trainer and know already what works for you.

Elliptical

Just get on an elliptical set at a low to moderate tension or level. Use the handles to get in a little upper body blood flow. Remember not to get your heart rate into the Training Zone. Try to stay below that in the Warm-up Zone.

Rowing Machine

A rowing machine has a little bit steeper learning curve than an elliptical. Sit down, fasten your feet, lean forward and grab the handle and pull the handle back while straightening your legs and using your glutes and lower back to lean back away from the spool while pulling the handle to your chest. It's a complicated motion for some. Remember not to curl forward or backward with your lower back muscles. Hinge at the hip, not the bottom of your ribs. Pull your elbows back and squeeze your shoulder blades together as the handle touches your chest. Don't exaggerate your motion using your wrists.

Jacob's Ladder

The Jacob's Ladder also has a bit of a learning curve. You'll need to fasten the belt, adjust the length of the strap going to the throttle on the machine, set it to your weight and then get on and start climbing. An alternated Left-Right Hand-Foot pattern will get you there. Mess around a bit and you should be able to figure it out. They have some YouTube videos to help you learn. Don't try anything fancy, keep your heart rate down and get the blood flowing. Do remember to keep a good arch in your lower back, without hunching over the rungs. Keeping your heart rate low on a Jacob's Ladder is pretty tough unless you go really slow or are in excellent cardio condition.

Walking Lunges

Un-weighted walking lunges are an excellent warm-up. If you can do them for 5:00 then it would be great. If you need to put a hand on top of each leg to give a little boost it wouldn't be so bad, especially in the Adjustment Cycle. You can also put your hands up, or behind your back for a bit of balance training. Remember this is not a workout, it's a warm-up so don't get your heart rate up too high. Usually that means go slowly and gently. If you can do weighted walking lunges with a low heart rate you're an advanced trainer for sure.

Box Stepping

Just what it sounds like. Get a box meant for this exercise. They are often called cardio boxes, aerobic platforms, plyometric boxes, jump boxes and probably lots of other things. It will be obvious that it's meant to carry a 200 pound + dynamic load. If you don't have one, or access to one, you can make do with something really sturdy to step up onto and down from. The landing on a stairway can work great. If you're really strong a park bench can work.

Just step up with one foot. Bring the other foot up next to it. Step down with one foot. Then take the other foot down. If you have balance issues you can use your trekking poles or a doorway or other type of support. Don't go leaning too heavily on your support. If your hands slip you'll fall and it will hurt quite a bit. Don't get fancy right now. Just up and down and up and down for 5:00 while keeping your heart rate below the training zone. That usually means go slow.

I myself prefer to use one leg at a time, say 100 with my left foot on the box and stepping up and down with my right foot, then switch feet and do another 100. It's up to you what works best.

For height, at first you might only be able to stay in the Warm-up zone with a 6" box and slowly work your way up to a 24" box. I like to use a metronome app on my phone to count beats. Start with 20 beats per minute and work your way up. I can set my metronome app to sound a counter-beat, so I have an up and down beat to follow with my foot. Of course, that's with my one-foot up and down, switch feet pattern. With a left up, right up, left down, right down pattern you'd have two up beats and two down beats. Make sense?

When to Use a Treadmill or Stepmill?

I would rather you not get in too much vertical in these warm-ups, so no Stepmill. After the adjustment period our weekly mileage goals can get quite extreme compared to during this first four week period. Then it would be greatly beneficial to do the warm-up and cool-down for about a half mile each on a flat (0% inclination) treadmill. If you look for the "with a Mileage Deduction for Strength Training" charts in the second half of the book you'll see how that works.

Core Training

Your core, as I've stated before, holds everything together. It's really important to get in a good core session every day of your training. I want you to get in about five minutes, 5:00, of basic training. I don't want these to be so intense that they affect your strength training, so use an easier variation if needed. On the other hand I do want them to be tough enough to cause growth in core strength and stability. Be honest with yourself and make it happen.

If possible, try to do about 0:20 (20 seconds) of each static hold, followed by 0:10 (10 seconds) of rest. Do 2 sets of each of the Planks. At first you might have to do sets of 0:10/:20 (hold/rest) but hopefully by the end of the Adjustment Cycle you'll be up to the 0:20/0:10. If you're an advanced trainer you could do 0:40/0:20 and only one set each. Note that the Side Plank is unilateral - you'll be doing 2 sets, one on each side, left and right.

Plank and Side Plank

Plank:

With your toes and elbows on the floor, straighten out your body and keep your spine and hips straight while staying in balance. You can go wide or narrow with your hands and feet, and you'll find the best position for you. If that's too easy go up on your hands or elevate your feet.

Side Plank:

With your feet crossed for comfort and one elbow on the floor straighten your hips and spine and stay facing forward. Hold that position for your time. If you want to make it more difficult raise your feet or go up on your hand instead of your elbow.

Summit Success

Reverse Plank and Superman Plank

Reverse Plank:

Lay on your back on the floor. Go up on your heels and elbows facing upward keeping your spine and hips straight. If you want to make it more difficult raise your feet or go up on your hands.

Superman Plank:

Lay on your stomach on the floor, extend your hands out over your head and lift your shoulders and knees off the floor looking like the classic superhero pose. Hold that position for your time. If this is too difficult just do reps for 0:01 (1 second) with a lot more rest. Break into it gently.

Summit Success

Strength Training Exercises

The following descriptions and illustrations show a simple version of the program. There are several different ways to do it, depending on whether you are at a commercial gym or on your own. It could then be further broken down into whether you already have equipment or not, and how much money you already have spent on equipment or want to budget on future equipment. The sky is the limit. I thought that in this sequence of illustrations I would try to stick to a handful of dumbbells and/or kettlebells and go from there.

If you are in a commercial gym, as I stated previously, there are several varieties of equipment that can do the same as these exercises. Remember that for this program we're not bodybuilding. We're just toning up your muscles to support your hiking. Don't do anything that repeatedly leaves you too sore to train. Once or twice during the adjustment cycle just so you can learn your limits and work past them. Otherwise do not get so sore you cannot train.

Romanian Deadlift

The Romanian Deadlift, sometimes called the Reverse Deadlift or Straight Leg Deadlift is deceptively simple. You basically reach down and pick up a weight at your feet then stand up all while keeping your legs relatively straight. If you haven't done this before start with Body Weight or non-weight like a plastic pipe or rubber ball or something for your first session to get the idea on how it moves.

Stand with feet about shoulder width apart and toes pointing forward. Hold your weight squarely in front of you along the top of your thighs. Keeping your chin up and out, and your shoulders square over your feet, hinge at the hips to extend out over your feet as you reach straight down to lower the weight. Now reverse the motion, keeping your back arched properly and in a good posture while letting the weight, imaginary or not, skim along the front of your legs as you unhinge your hips visualizing pushing your navel to the front. Just lower it gently to the floor following the reverse of your motion. You need to train the Eccentric for your downhill hiking endurance.

Remember to keep your chin out and forward and your lower back in the proper arch. Do not hunch.

Example Training Journal Entry:

Romanian Deadlift: 10 @ 135 lb./BW x 3

Example illustrated is the Dumbbell Romanian Deadlift. Keep the lower back neutral and the chin tilted forward.

Summit Success

Training for Hiking, Mountaineering, and Peak Bagging – by Charles Miske

Squat

The Squat is the foundation of leg strength. You have just done Deadlifts so you'll be a little bit weaker than if you were doing Squats first. This is okay because we're more interested in endurance than in raw strength.

Stand with your heels about shoulder width and your toes pointing outward at about 45 degrees. This is the same position as in the Deep Squat Static Stretch we did earlier. If you set your feet up at about that same position you should be fine.

The motion is almost identical as well, only if you're using a barbell your elbows will be outside your knees. If you've never done Squats before then start with just Body Weight at first. If you can't do 3 sets of 10 at Body Weight you shouldn't be using a barbell. There are several variations of Squat to work your way up in strength and resistance.

Be alert and aware for any types of pain in any joint or location. In general it means your position is incorrect. If you have never done squats before I do recommend that you do a variation referred to as "Sissy Squat". If you go to my website http://sevensummits-body.com/summitsuccess page you'll see that I've posted several articles about it over the years. It's a great warm-up and general mobility exercise.

Quickly, grab the edge of a countertop and with a little bit of arm support stick your bottom out and lower it over your heels until your thighs (front tops of legs) are roughly parallel to the ground. Keep your back as straight as you can. Then using your hands and arms gently rise up to standing. Do 3 sets of 10 of those if you are able. If that's the most you can do, good deal. Do those for your strength training for now.

Example Training Journal Entry:

Squat: 10 @ 135 lb./BW x 3

Example illustrated is a Dumbbell Goblet Squat, holding the dumbbell in both hands in front of the chest, and lowering down till thighs are parallel to the floor. Return up. Keep the lower back safe and neutral, even though there isn't much weight involved.

Training for Hiking, Mountaineering, and Peak Bagging – by Charles Miske

Summit Success

Pull-down or Chin-up

You will need strong back muscles to support using trekking poles as you work your way both uphill and downhill. If you can't do Chin-ups or Pull-ups, then you'll have to do Lat Pull-downs instead.

I'll explain the Chin-up and Pull-up first. Classically you just grab a bar over your head with your palms facing away from you (Pull-up) or facing each other or you (Chin-up). Lift your feet and lift yourself until your chin is at about the level of your hands, above or below a little either way. Lower yourself under control until your elbows are almost straight. You don't need to unhinge your shoulders. Try to keep your shoulders straight across and don't let them raise up toward your ears at the bottom. This is more important for some people than others so be careful. It can cause shoulder pain if you let your shoulders go with an exaggerated Range of Motion.

Kipping, or flinging your knees and feet up, is a way to cheat a Pull-up. I'm not going to keep you from doing it if that's what you have to do to get in your sets and reps. But work toward not having to Kip as a way to increase strength.

If you need assistance at a level more than what you would get from Kipping but are generally able to do your Pull-ups then you can use a slightly lower bar and bounce off your toes a little between reps. If you need even more assistance then see if you have access to an assisted Pull-up machine like the Gravitron. If not then you might be able to do them in a Power Rack with a large tubing or band between pins to kneel or stand on to help effectively reduce your weight. Progress can be measured by using less or no assistance of any kind, including Kipping. If that's all over your head then by all means, find someone to show you or just do Lat Pull-downs.

With a Lat Pull-down you sit in a bench with your knees locked into pads and pull down a horizontal bar from above and use a Selectorized Weight Stack to set the amount of resistance. Note that most, if not all of these machines with the weight stacks have some leverage, so if it says 60 pounds on the stack it might be only 15 or 20 or 30 pounds. It's only relevant if you are going to become a competitive Lat Pull-down champion. Otherwise for your Training Journal just note the number on the side of the plate and make progress by using more plates.

If you are at home then you can use rubber bands or tubes set into a doorway for Lat Pull-downs or a doorway bar for Pull-ups.

Example Training Journal Entries:

Lat Pull-down: 10 @ 135 lb./Band x 3

Chin-up: 10 @ BW x 3 (note any assistance)

Gravitron Pull-up: 10 @ BW - 80 lb. x 3

Example illustrated is the Selectorized Machine Lat Pull-down. The first photo is sitting in the bench with the legs under the supports provided, holding onto the bar connected to the cable with hands about 6" wider than shoulder width and palms facing away. The second photo shows pulling the bar to the mid-chest level without exaggerating the motion with bent wrists, which is quite common. Keep the back arched properly and the chin up to align the spine.

Training for Hiking, Mountaineering, and Peak Bagging – by Charles Miske

Summit Success

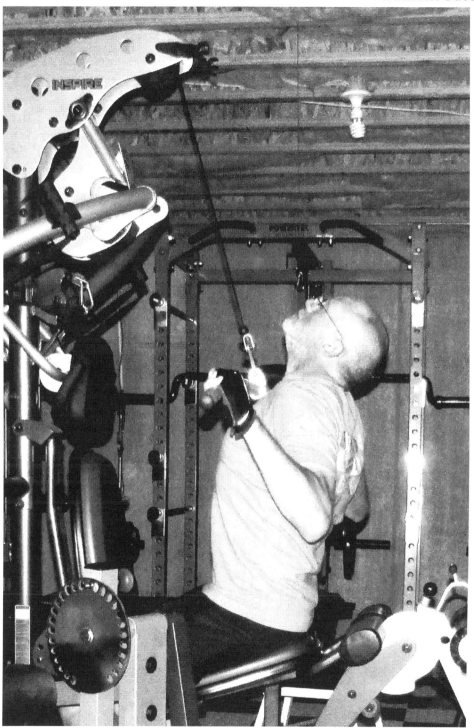

Row

Rowing is also a back workout to develop the supporting muscles for using trekking poles while hiking no steep trails. You can do these unilaterally. You could also do these as Bent Over Rows with a barbell.

To do Unilaterally, or one side at a time, set one knee and one hand on a bench, or prop your hand on your knee, and with the free hand, grab a dumbbell and while leaning forward with your back in proper posture, lift your elbow up and to the rear. Think of pulling your elbows up behind you, not pulling the weight to your chest. Otherwise you might try for too much range of motion and try using your wrist for extra pulling. This can cause wrist issues so don't do it.

Crank out your 10 reps and without wasting a lot of time switch sides and crank out 10 on that side. Keep switching, 3 sets on each side. It should only take a couple minutes longer to do it this way.

If you have a barbell just lean forward hinging at the hips, keeping your back in good posture, like the bottom forward position in the Good Morning. Lift the bar to your chest by pulling your elbows to the rear. Be sure to be safe with your back.

Example Training Journal Entries:

Bent Over Row: 10 @ 135 lb. x 3

Dumbbell Row: 10 ea. @ 40 lb. x 3

Example illustrated is the Unilateral Dumbbell Row. Brace yourself on your bent opposite knee in a lunge position, bring your elbow up to the side maintaining a neutral wrist.

Summit Success

Training for Hiking, Mountaineering, and Peak Bagging – by Charles Miske

Chest

For Chest, if you have a Bench Press bench and rack, like in a gym, and know what to do on your own, then do the Bench Press. If not, you can do the Floor Press. If you're at home and strong you can do Pushups.

The chest is an Antagonist Muscle for the back. We're training it only a little to help support strength growth in the back and prevent injury. We're not going to focus too much on it.

Floor Press is done laying on your back on the floor, as the name implies. Take two dumbbells, one in each hand, and with your hands straight above your elbows, press the weight up and toward the ceiling, letting your hands track inward so that the weights are straight above your shoulders. Reverse that path to return to the start. Repeat for reps.

Pushups can be difficult for many people. If you can't do them then please get some dumbbells and do the Floor Press. Lay on your front on the floor and push your toes into the floor. Put your hands on the floor a little over shoulder width apart and in a line with the base of your sternum. This is a decent start for a Pushup position. If you find yourself wanting to put your hands at ear height and way out away from your body it means you're probably not strong enough for Pushups. You can work your way into it by balancing on your knees instead of your toes. If you're still not strong enough to do 3 sets of 10 then go back to the Floor Press. Be honest with yourself and prevent injury. It's not a contest.

Example Training Journal Entries:

Floor Press: 10 @ 40 lb. x 3

Pushup: 10 @ BW x 3

Example illustrated is the Dumbbell Floor Press. Keep the dumbbells over your elbows at the bottom and bring them slightly toward each other at the top.

Training for Hiking, Mountaineering, and Peak Bagging – by Charles Miske

Summit Success

Shoulders

The shoulder exercise I'd like for you to do is essentially a Unilateral Tri-Set. Three exercises performed on each side, one after the other. It's a dynamic exercise but you'll be using light weights. If you're an advanced trainer, just relax and try these for a few weeks, considering them as a functional mobility circuit. Then you can go back to whatever it is you've been doing.

Begin in a neutral stance, feet somewhere between together and shoulder width apart. Keep you back straight and arms loosely straight at the sides. Use whatever weights you have. You could even use bags of sand, medicine or other weighted balls.

First, take a dumbbell or kettle bell and swing it up in the air to the front with just a little bit of body English. Remember to keep your back in good posture. Keep your knees and hips flexed. Swing it up to about horizontal or slightly above. There isn't much benefit to going any higher. Do not go back past your hips on the side. Be careful not to hit yourself. Do 10 and then switch sides.

Second, swing the weight straight out to the side at about parallel with your stance. Bring it in at the bottom past your hip and almost to your navel and immediately take it back out to the side. Don't go too high and don't hit yourself. Also resist the temptation to use the other hand to "push" the weight up and out. Repeat on the other side.

Third, swing to the rear while keeping your back straight upright. Don't worry too much about height. Your own shoulder mobility will restrict it somewhat. Don't let it go past your hip to the front. Switch sides.

That's the shoulder circuit I would like you to try. It's actually kind of fun. Just be sure to not use too much body English or momentum to drive the weight up and out. Also don't get hit. It hurts.

Example Training Journal Entry:

Shoulder Circuit 10 ea. @ 30 lb. x 3

Example illustrated is the Dumbbell 3-way Shoulder Circuit in four photos. First is the neutral standing position, second the front swing, third the side swing, and fourth the rear swing. Remember to keep moving while doing this exercise. You can use kettle bells instead if you have some.

Summit Success

Training for Hiking, Mountaineering, and Peak Bagging – by Charles Miske

Training for Hiking, Mountaineering, and Peak Bagging – by Charles Miske

Calf Raise

Calf Raise is a pretty simple workout. Stand on the floor, on the edge of a step, or edge of a block of something stable. Keep your balance, using your trekking poles if needed and use your calf muscles, not momentum, to lift yourself to the maximum extension. Hold it for a second then return to the starting position. You might see articles about how to bend and turn your feet to different angles, but that isn't really necessary, especially at the beginning of your training. Those articles are more for bodybuilders who want to make sure their calf muscles are nice and round. We don't care what shape they are so long as they do the job.

If these are too easy, and you don't feel anything at all doing a set of 10 then you can either add weight or try them unilaterally. If you need to add weight you could even just stuff your backpack and use that for extra weight. Or hang onto some weight plates, dumbbells or kettle bells. If you are just starting out I prefer you not use a barbell at this time, since it can cause balance issues. Get a few hundred sets behind you then try the barbell. You could also do these on one foot at a time, if you feel comfortable with the balance. If you need to touch something like a wall or trekking pole for comfort and security that's fine, just don't crank on them to help your calf muscles at all.

Also avoid bending your knees and using the large muscles of your upper leg to get a boost upward. That takes away a lot of the benefit of doing them. Your calf muscles are very important for stepping uphill since pushing off with your toes on steep terrain involves the calf muscles heavily. Do it near the end, because of the type of muscle fiber and how it might affect your other leg training if you do it before.

Example Training Journal Entry:

Calf Raise: 25 @ BW x 3

Example illustrated is a Body Weight Calf Raise using a dumbbell as a toe platform. It was handy. You can use stairs or boards or steps. Anything to get your toes up a couple inches that is stable enough to support your body in motion.

Training for Hiking, Mountaineering, and Peak Bagging – by Charles Miske

Summit Success

Biceps & Triceps

Biceps and Triceps are supporting muscles for your forearms and shoulders for using the trekking poles while hiking. They're not that important in the big scheme of things, but will help you make better and faster progress in your other Strength Training, especially Pushups and Pull-ups. Since they are only supporting exercises and done last, I'm combining them. Do 3 sets of 10 mixing it up however you want. You can do 3 sets of one and alternate them between workouts doing one on the first strength training day, and the other on the second strength training day of each week in the cycle. You can do two of one and one of the other, alternating on each strength training day. It's up to you how to mix them up, just be sure to log it and keep track of progress.

I almost don't have to describe them, they're so basic to everything you've ever seen on TV or Magazines, articles and ads.

For the Biceps Curl just take a weight and without moving your shoulders or elbow, lift it up near your shoulder and then reverse the path and return it to your side. Try not to use body English or momentum. Just up and down. It's that simple. After your reps are done for that set switch sides and repeat. Continue on for your sets and reps.

Example Training Journal Entry:

Dumbbell Biceps Curl: 10 ea. @ 30 lb. x 3

Example illustrated is the Dumbbell Biceps Curl. Let the dumbbells swing up to your shoulders while keeping your elbows in one place.

Summit Success

Training for Hiking, Mountaineering, and Peak Bagging – by Charles Miske

Summit Success

For the Triceps you might have a bit more trouble. If you're at a commercial gym you can use a Selectorized Weight Stack Tower with a rope handle set at about chest height. Grab the rope in both hands and keeping your back straight and hinged at the hips, press the handle down toward the front of your legs and then let the rope return up and repeat.

If you're at home you can use rubber bands in your doorway just as you would with the machine above. You could also do Triceps Kickbacks. Stand as though you were doing the Unilateral Dumbbell Row as previously. Lift your elbow up and to the rear with the weight hanging straight down toward the floor.

Using the Triceps extend the dumbbell to the rear without moving your elbow from your side. Let the weight gently return to the bottom and repeat. Switch sides and do it again. Repeat until you get in your sets.

Example Training Journal Entry:

Dumbbell Triceps Kickback: 10 ea. @ 30 lb. x 3

Examples illustrated:

First the Dumbbell Triceps Kickback. Bend forward with the dumbbell near your waist with your elbow high. Keeping your elbow still swing the dumbbell up to the rear. On the way down don't let the dumbbell swing forward of your waist toward your chest to add momentum.

Training for Hiking, Mountaineering, and Peak Bagging – by Charles Miske

Summit Success

For the next example, we're doing the Dumbbell Overhead Triceps Press. For this exercise stand in the neutral position with your hand holding your weight over and behind your head slightly. If you have a selectorized tower with cables or even bands you can do this with the cable or bands running down behind your back.

Be careful not to hurt your elbow, so you'll have to watch your motion to make sure your arm extends to the side an appropriate distance to protect it.

Next extend your hand holding the weight or cable or band straight up over your head. This will use your shoulder somewhat so if you have shoulder issues the previous Triceps Kickbacks might be a better option.

Examples Illustrated:

Second, the Dumbbell Triceps Overhead Press. Set the dumbbell just above your shoulder with your elbow extended out toward the front. Keeping your shoulder relatively still, without unnecessary movement, use your triceps muscle to press the dumbbell toward the ceiling. Lower under control.

Summit Success

Training for Hiking, Mountaineering, and Peak Bagging – by Charles Miske

Strength Training Outside with Bands

Shortly after my Beta Testers (guinea pigs) started the program I received some questions about how to train on the cheap and outside. It seriously changed the entire structure of the program and this is one of the results. It's understandable that someone who wants to excel in hiking and mountaineering skills would want to spend as much time outside as possible and not inside a gym. Also, sometimes gyms aren't convenient or are expensive. It depends sometimes on the level of competition in a local area.

I'm doing most of the strength training exercises shown in the previous section with bands or bodyweight. The bands I'm using here are the EliteFTS Pro Bands and are available between $5 and $15 depending on the resistance level. That's at the time of the printing of the first edition (September 2014).

In this series of photos I'm using a Pro Micro Mini Band wherever two long bands are used, like Biceps, Triceps, and Shoulders. I'm using a Pro Mini Band for the Pull-Downs. I'm using a Pro Monster Mini Band for the RDL, Squat and Bent Over Row. That's just in case you want to duplicate what I have done here.

In general, if you get two each of those lighter bands you'll spend something around $65 and you can always double up bands if you're really strong. You can also make them shorter by choking up on them (holding them somewhere other than the end) which is also good for your grip. You could fold them so they have half the range of motion and twice the resistance. The next heavier bands have a lot more resistance.

A caveat, and a major one for some people is that while it does provide resistance it's not weight. There's a very subtle difference there. You can't measure your progress so easily unless you start adding in reps. You could work your way up to a few hundred triceps presses, but that's time consuming. You could start adding up more and more bands. In general though if all you want is a "toning" type strength training session, in which you're doing "work" and aren't too concerned otherwise, count it as a great alternative to the gym.

The best part is that they all fit in your little hiking backpack, or even the large front pocket of a hoodie, like the one I'm wearing in the photos. Do a 10 minute warm-up walk, whip out the bands and get it done. Then do a 10 minute walk back home or to the car and it's all good.

Plank & Side Plank

There's not a lot different with a plank done outside except watch out for mud, muck, metal bits, glass bits, droppings, etc.

Summit Success

159

Reverse Plank & Superman Plank

Since your back is to the ground in a Reverse Plank, and your tummy and other sensitive areas are on the ground in the Superman Plank you need to be extra careful about checking the area you'll be training in. Be safe.

Summit Success

Romanian Deadlift

Start with the Romanian Deadlift as before. Lay the band under your feet and grasp the loops. Adjust it so that the ends are even. Keep your back straight and hinge at the hips. Be sure you end the motion upright with your shoulders squarely over your feet.

Summit Success

Squat

The Band Squat is a little odd feeling at first. You might feel really off balance but keep your weight and shoulders directly over your feet and trust that it will work.

Stand on the middle of the band with your feet about shoulder width apart and toes pointed outward. If you've done bodyweight squats it will be the same position. Squat down and grab the loops of band, making sure it's even on both sides. Stand up. Keep your hands near the front sides of your legs.

Summit Success

Pull-Down

This is an odd variation, but is essentially the same thing as the Lat Pull-down on a machine as shown previously. I'm wrapping a tree trunk but it would work as well on anything above your head. Lean forward and hinge at the hips with a flat back and reach straight out.

I'm leaning my center of gravity back from the band. If I let go of it I'd probably fall backward. Keeping your weight back do the pull-down motion trying to keep your hands holding the bands in line with your ears. There's no point in rotating your wrists for that last quarter inch range of motion. When you feel like turning your wrists that's the stopping point. Then repeat. Alert: don't fall over if you try this one.

Summit Success

Row

The Bent Over Row is one of the simple obvious ones. Stand on the center of the band, lean forward hinged at the hips. Grab the loops, making sure they're even and pull your elbows straight back.

Summit Success

Chest

You could drape a band over your shoulders and grasp the loops if you want more resistance. But most normal introductory level strength trainers would do well enough to get in what amounts to 30 push-ups in just a few minutes. So my outside example is a simple push-up done in the grass. Watch out for glass, metal, and droppings, please.

Summit Success

Shoulders

I'm going to show this from a few different angles just to make sure you have it down. This is the 3-Way Shoulder exercise I described previously, only done with bands for resistance. For this one you use two bands. I'm using the lightest, least expensive bands. If you need more resistance choke up on the band. I'll show you that in an upcoming pic. There is a pretty long range of motion on this exercise, from your feet up to the limits of your upward reach. Stand with your toes in the loops with the band under the ball of your foot or instep.

Front: grab the loops in front of your hips and swing your arms up to the front, keeping your elbows slightly bent. Don't go for too far of a range of motion. The extra few degrees of rotation aren't all the productive or functional.

Side: just like the front, only start with your hands out to the side, about 45 degrees out from your hips. Swing your arms out to the side. Again, don't go for an extreme range of motion.

Side: this is another view of the side, so you can see where the hands begin and end their motion from another angle. This should make it easier to duplicate for yourself.

Rear: the most complicated of the shoulder exercises with the band. To get an appropriate range of motion you'll begin leaning forward, hinged at the hips. Keep your back flat and neutral as you swing your arms to the rear within your own comfort range. Since you have to clear your own body with the band you'll have to start in a slightly wider position than with the other two shoulder motions. It shouldn't hurt. You'll know pretty much right away. This is actually pretty important for supporting the back and chest muscles while going downhill with trekking poles.

Summit Success

Training for Hiking, Mountaineering, and Peak Bagging – by Charles Miske

Summit Success

Training for Hiking, Mountaineering, and Peak Bagging – by Charles Miske

Summit Success

Calf Raise

I found a flat square rock that was pretty balanced and tested it first to see if it would tip. It seemed sound enough for doing single leg (unilateral) calf raises so I did them. If you are having balance issues please use trekking poles or even the trunk of a tree and you will feel a lot more stable. If you're going to do both legs together it's probably a little easier for balance. I love the challenge though and it's a good workout.

I'm showing three photos. In the first I'm keeping my arms close to my body for less assistance in balancing.

In the second I'm holding my arms out further for balance.

Notice that in both photos I go pretty far down with my heel to stretch my calf muscle and increase the range of motion. You don't have to go quite so far. Go for your own optimum range of motion.

In the third photo I show a closer view so you can see the range of motion.

From the lowest position of my heel to the highest is about 4-6". That's not a lot. Don't push it or you might end up with cramps, sometimes even a few days later.

Training for Hiking, Mountaineering, and Peak Bagging – by Charles Miske

Summit Success

Training for Hiking, Mountaineering, and Peak Bagging – by Charles Miske

Biceps

Stand on a loop of two bands, grab the loop and while keeping your elbows tucked in at your sides, lift your hands to your shoulders.

In this case I'm choking up on the bands, or holding them further along than the end of the loop. This is to make the bands shorter. That increases the resistance some, but most importantly gives me resistance along the entire range of motion. If I hold the ends the band is slack until about halfway through the movement.

Training for Hiking, Mountaineering, and Peak Bagging – by Charles Miske

Triceps

This is another tricky one until you get the hang of it. Stand with your heels over the loop of the band and grab the other end with your hands behind your back and flip it up over behind your head with your hands near your shoulders. Good thing I show these photos, hey?

Keep your elbows lined up diagonally out over your shoulders as you lift the bands behind your head and reach for a position straight up over your head.

I show three views for this photo so you can see the elbows out in the middle of the motion so you can see how it works. This is dependent on your own shoulder and elbow mobility so yours might look a bit different from mine. But you get the idea, right?

Training for Hiking, Mountaineering, and Peak Bagging – by Charles Miske

184

Strength Training Outside Wrapping Up

So there you have a quick look at what it might be like to do your strength training routine outside with about $50 in equipment. Instead of bands, I've seen people using sliced up bicycle inner tubes. That might work if you have a cycling friend who collects flat tubes. You'd be surprised how many of us put them in a box so they can fix them someday while watching reality TV.

This routine takes about a half hour to do if you don't rest a lot between things, and most of it is pretty easy to set up.

Training for Hiking, Mountaineering, and Peak Bagging – by Charles Miske

General Hiking and Mountaineering Info

While you're working out for your Four Week Adjustment Cycle I'd like to share a few thoughts about hiking, mountaineering, training and some general information that will be of benefit to you in your upcoming adventures. First I'd like to share something that I feel is of utmost importance when you venture into the outdoors and wild places - The Leave No Trace Seven Principles - an excellent set of guidelines to help you make wise decisions to reduce your impact.

Next I'll share some information with you about training with a backpack on and how to fit it into the program. We'll discuss shoes, socks, rainwear, trekking poles and the other essentials for your upcoming hike.

Photo, next page, is from a trail run overlooking the Keystone Resort Ranches Golf Course with possible trail connectors to the Colorado Trail. You can just make out the classic prominent summit of Buffalo Mountain over my right shoulder, a 12'er.

Summit Success

Training for Hiking, Mountaineering, and Peak Bagging – by Charles Miske

Leave No Trace Principles

I don't want you to go out into the wilderness in Colorado, or any other state, and leave it in worse condition than you found it. The sad fact is that for so many years those that have gone before us on the trails figured that the wilderness was a giant black hole and anything you dumped into it would blow away or decompose fast enough that no one would ever notice.

When I was on Carstensz Pyramid there was a huge dump at base camp. The stuff there was a mix of stuff, but a lot of it wouldn't have been practical to haul up the 6 day trek in a porter's bag. There was a jeep road nearby but to drive on it would be trespassing on private land. Very sad state of affairs in one of the most wild and scenic parts of the whole world.

Please don't contribute to the destruction of our wild lands. As a Boy Scout Leader I've had the opportunity to teach my young campers the Leave No Trace Seven Principles, as outlined in this chapter. I highly recommend that you visit their website and read the materials there to help you make wise decisions in how you can help to prevent further damage to our valuable wild areas.

The Colorado 14ers are one of the most visited hiking destinations in the state and there are a lot of people there who have no idea about the potential damage they are doing to our mountains. Don't be one of them.

Aside from the common sense of pack it in, pack it out, seriously consider the impact of human waste on the environment. Find the website for the government agency in charge of the area in which you'll be hiking and read up on the rules for human waste management. On Mount Rainier, as an example, above certain camps, you are required to use plastic bags, available at the ranger stations, and dispose of the full bags in appointed bins at a few choice locations.

Photo, next page, is the garbage strewn around the Carstensz Pyramid Base Camp.

Summit Success

Training for Hiking, Mountaineering, and Peak Bagging – by Charles Miske

The Leave No Trace Seven Principles.

1 - Plan Ahead and Prepare

2 - Travel and Camp on Durable Surfaces

3 - Dispose of Waste Properly

4 - Leave What You Find

5 - Minimize Campfire Impacts

6 - Respect Wildlife

7 - Be Considerate of Other Visitors

The member-driven Leave No Trace Center for Outdoor Ethics teaches people how to enjoy the outdoors responsibly. This copyrighted information has been reprinted with permission from the Leave No Trace Center for Outdoor Ethics: www.LNT.org.

I do have a few thoughts about these that I'd like to share. I mentioned before that you should find out what rules apply to the trail you'd like to hike on. Some trails have rules about fire and water and human waste, but there are also rules about dogs including dog waste removal and leash requirements. I've been tripped many times by dogs on too long a leash for them to be under control as well as dogs wandering around free and loose in places where they are not allowed. Dog waste is common all along the trails I run on, and it's an unsightly mess that smells pretty bad and attracts insects and other pests. Please be a responsible pet owner. In the big scheme of things this is to help you to keep the trails open for other dog owners. It might take only one serious incident to get the trails closed permanently.

There is way too much garbage along the trails as well. I see lots of candy bar and granola bar wrappers, as well as plastic disposable bottles. Please manage your trash. It only takes a few seconds and an ounce or two to keep your trash on you until you get to a proper place to dispose of it. Even the pull tabs from goo packets are too common along the trails. The little foil bottle seals, juice box straw wrappers, toothpick wrappers, and lots of other tiny little stuff litters the trail, and all it takes is a glint of shiny sunlight from the right angle to reveal it all. Don't leave it for others, or Mother Nature who might be able to dissolve it to dust in a thousand years or so.

I normally keep all my snacks in a larger zipper seal bag. When I'm done with my snack wrappers I fold them neatly and place them back inside. I fold the goo packets with the opening and tear strip in the center to keep the bag from becoming sticky from the residue. You could try this system at first and see what works best for you.

Summit Success

Too many people are souvenir collectors. Take pictures, not a summit rock or plant. In some areas it can be a federal offense to collect a trophy. Don't even snag a stick from along the trail to use as a walking stick or cane in accordance with some 19th century tradition of the jolly good stroll with the boys. In the same vein, it's disruptive when a group of kids runs down the sides of the trail waving sticks and throwing rocks at each other and screaming in some misplaced game. That's what soccer fields are for.

Many times I've been up Quandary, a popular Colorado 14er and seen mountain goats and pika along the trail. I cut them a lot of slack. They live there. I don't. I've seen kids chasing the pika and marmots and chipmunks. I've seen dozens of people trying to get within touching distance of the goats. As used to humans as they seem to be, they are still wild creatures and can be unpredictable at best. Leave them alone please. Take some distant photos and enjoy them with your friends and family.

As far as consideration of others, I've seen several groups splayed out along the trail preventing anyone from possibly making uphill or downhill progress without tripping over them. It's even worse when it's at a steep and rough section. It might look like a great place to rest, but if you can hang on for a few more minutes or twenty, there will be a great wide flat spot just made for taking a break. The people doing it generally seem ignorant that anyone would want to go around them and that they are in the way. They get all mad at you and even say rude comments when someone interrupts their rest. Don't be those people.

Hopefully these few ideas and suggestions won't offend you. It's best though if you don't represent any of the examples. Go for peace and harmony on the trail with your fellow hikers all of whom are in their own zone and have their own reasons for being on the mountain. Some will be trail runners working on setting a PR for their ascent or car-to-car times. Some will be wearing huge boots and 50 lb. packs training for Everest or Denali. Some will have sweet camera gear and trying for that perfect photo. Some will be hanging out for a day of adventure with friends. Some want to be just left alone. Some want to talk to everyone they pass. I've both met and been several of those people over the years. They can be pretty cool if you let them, much of the time.

Enjoy it all and try to help out the future generations by making as little negative impact as possible. If you have the energy and drive then maybe you can even add in some of your own positive energy. Take a garbage sack with you and gather up everything. Take two, one for trash and one for recycling. Wear disposable gloves and carry hand sanitizer. Wear a white Nomex suit and give everyone a scare if that appeals to you. Whatever you do though, please, make a difference, one way or another.

Training for Hiking, Mountaineering, and Peak Bagging – by Charles Miske

The Backpack

Remember the backpack we discussed earlier? If you don't already own one, I need you to get a backpack before we begin the main program. Just a small one. You'll only need a few things in it, so it doesn't need to be very big. Some type of insulated jacket, a windbreaker, a hat and gloves and a couple bandanas. A one-gallon zip lock of snacks and a few liters of water. This will weigh at most about 15 pounds. At most. A school book bag type backpack will work, but if you need to get a new hiking or trekking backpack, see about something in the 12-20 liter range. This is the measurement of internal capacity.

Your backpack will be where all of the stuff you're not currently carrying will go. I'd rather you don't strap stuff all over the outside as you'll see some people doing. Clattering around on the outside, swinging freely, your items are likely to bump into you and cause great annoyance, or worse, bump into a fellow hiker. It could get stuck on brush, yanking you back and causing even more annoyance. If you fall it could turn into the classic "Yard Sale" with your items strewn about the trail. Just stick it all into that backpack.

In the big scheme of things, it doesn't matter too much what type or size you have, so long as it's big enough to carry your items but not so big that it causes you irritation. A big empty pack flopping about on your back will get old really quick. If it's all you have, and you can cinch down all the adjustment straps to effectively turn it into a smaller pack, then fine, go ahead.

Otherwise, a simple inexpensive pack will do the job. I prefer fewer pockets, having developed my own organizing system over the years, but you might like a few pockets in which to place your snacks and emergency supplies, just in case. If you're going to use a water bladder, then make sure there is a pocket or connectors to hang you bladder in or on, depending on the style of bladder you use, and that there is an opening on your preferred drinking side. There should also be an elastic or Velcro strap to hold your tube to the shoulder strap. As I stated previously, a child's school bag will do it. Cartoon characters are always a topic of interesting discussion on the trails, if you want a good opening line.

"Dude, I love the Hello Kitty backpack!"

I also would like it if it were the same backpack you train in. At least a few times in your training, load it up with the gear you'll be using on your adventures and see how it all fits. Make sure the straps are all adjusted correctly. In general, you want the waistband to sit on your Iliac Crest, the crescent shaped bone above your hip joint. This will take some of the weight off your shoulders. It will be very important after five or so hours on the trail.

Summit Success

You want to be able to easily slide a couple of fingers under the top of the shoulder strap when the backpack is fully loaded. You don't want a lot of weight pulling down on your shoulder/neck muscles. It will make you feel a lot more tired than you really are.

As far as training with it goes, I don't need to make a chart because this is quite simple. For week one, just wear the backpack for all your cardio. Then each week up to week 16 just add in a pound of stuff. Cans of food or bottles of water work. I've used empty juice bottles, weighed them on a scale and added water to them to make my training weight. Don't overthink this. By week 16 your bag will weigh about 15 pounds, and that's what we're shooting for.

If your training backpack is a bit floppy with whatever weighted objects are inside just stick in a small pillow or jacket or something to keep it from sliding around. I like to use the small camping or guest bed pillows.

Photo, next page, is with my backpack while trekking on the Horcones Trail to Aconcagua Base Camp. I trained with a 55 pound pack for this adventure, but do not recommend it without a solid base built up in weighted backpack training.

Photo, page following, is a typical daypack, about 15-20 liters in size. On the floor beside it are trekking poles. These collapse into a fairly small size rather quickly, but you don't need anything quite so fancy.

Training for Hiking, Mountaineering, and Peak Bagging – by Charles Miske

Summit Success

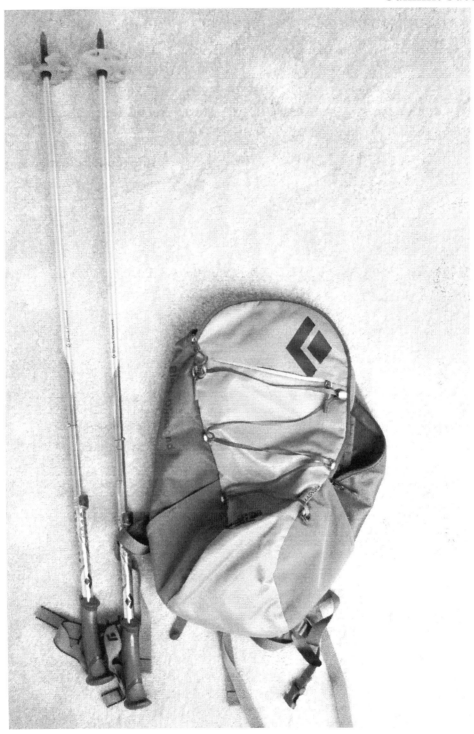

Training for Hiking, Mountaineering, and Peak Bagging – by Charles Miske

Gear for Hiking and Mountaineering for the Beginner

This is a good time for you to dig around in your gear and begin experimenting with what you have. You can train in your clothes and shoes, and stuff your backpack with all the goodies you'll be taking with on your hike. Remember that full water bottles are an excellent source of weight to bring your backpack up to the target weight.

If you are missing something, or it's broken this is a good time to buy, replace or repair what you need. I'd rather see you going with the least risk possible, which implies relatively new items that you train with to ensure that they are in working order. Best is to make sure they work for you.

This is especially important with clothes and shoes. You don't want blisters or raw feet from your shoes. You don't want sore knees or ankles from ill-fitting shoes or insoles. You don't want to get chafing or numbness where your clothes might be constricting. You don't want to be unable to get into and out of your weather clothing under harsh conditions. It's hard to imagine how that works. If you really want to test it, pull your hat down over your eyes, put on your backpack, put on mittens. Now get into your shower under a stream of cold water. Take off your backpack, put on your rain gear, and put your backpack on again. How much fun was that? Yeah. Thought you'd say that.

How about your snacks and food and water? Will the food you want to use actually work for you? One way to find out is to pack them on your hour long hikes near the end of the program. If you can pull them out and eat them and stuff the wrapper back in your pocket or backpack without breaking your stride they work great. If you don't get sick after eating them that's a definite plus. This is a bit extreme though. In the big hike at the end, your goal hike, you'll be stopping every hour for a few minutes to eat and drink.

That's a technique tip for you. When you're doing a big hike or climb, be sure to schedule in a stop about once an hour for 5:00. Stop, add or subtract layers as needed. Eat and drink quickly. With practice you can determine your needs and drink what you have available. As an example, if you have a 32 oz. Nalgene and you're going to stop 8 times, drink 4 oz. per stop. There are markings on the side of the bottle for you to do just that. Same with your snacks. If you plan to stop 8 times, bring 8 simple snacks. Eat one at every stop. If you're going home-made then put them in little baggies or other containers in single serving sizes.

Shoes, Boots and Socks

When I was in my teens and twenties I wore running shoes for almost all of my hiking adventures, including those that involved scrambling on rocks and loose slippery stuff like moss, gravel, scree and dirt. In my thirties I wore switched to half shank (metal or plastic plate inside the sole of the boot for stiffness and support - half generally means from the instep to the heel). I evolved over the next twenty years to now wearing trail running shoes with very thin insoles for almost all of my hiking, including on snow and ice with crampons. If I'm not actually climbing with ice tools or an ice axe, and it's above zero degrees Fahrenheit, I'll be in running shoes now. Here's my own evolution, in order.

- Running shoes
- Stiff half shank mid-height hikers
- Mid-height running shoe style hikers
- Low running shoe style hikers
- Waterproof heavy trail running shoes
- Light trail running shoes

I've come full circle it seems over a forty year period. I don't actually recommend this for anyone who is not also currently running several miles a week on a regular basis. If you have strong ankle and foot support tendons and ligaments, then you could try. If it's all you have and you don't want to fork over $200 or more for a pair of quality boots, then you could also try.

If all you can do is get in $50 or so for a pair of knock-off light hikers, my own personal opinion is that you can get a closeout on a pair of quality trail running shoes in the colors left over from last year for that same price range and be much better off. That's just my personal opinion though. Do what's best for you.

I do have to qualify that opinion though by saying that I do not know your own circumstance, your strengths and weaknesses, and your medical history, so obviously use some common sense and make smart choices for you and your circumstances. That being said, as I mentioned previously, I've seen people in flip flops and sandals doing the 14ers here in Colorado. So it can be done.

Boots, especially leather or synthetic leather, can offer more protection from rocks and brush with stiffer soles and, depending on the height, offer some level of ankle support in sideways moving loose terrain. That can come at the price of being generally harder to break in and having more material in contact with your ankles to cause potential blisters or scrapes rubbed raw by seams.

Fit then is ultimately the most important criterion in purchasing any footwear, whether leather, synthetic, fabric, weave, netting or even straps. My favorite trick is to take out the removable insole and stand on it with your heel placed firmly into the heel cup. If your toes hang over the front anywhere, the shoe is too short. If your big or little toes hang over the sides, especially at the toe and foot joints, the shoe is too narrow. A trick a guide once told me is to get a shoe or boot that fits, then fill the gaps with socks.

Always try them on in person in a store if you can. Some online retailers have great free return policies, so you could get the three sizes surrounding what you think will be your size and then return any that don't work.

For socks, lots of seasoned hikers like the wool blend socks with thick loop cushioning. Many companies offer them in various thicknesses, from thickest to thinnest cushioning:
- Mountaineering or Summit
- Trekking
- Hiking
- Walking
- Running

Many hikers also like a layer to help prevent sweat from accumulating close to their skin, or to prevent friction hot spots or blisters. If you get blisters between your toes there are also the toe-socks made by several manufacturers in different materials.

Old-school hikers like Ragg Wool Socks but I find them slow to dry, not as warm as the loop cushion socks and to me they feel like the hot spots of friction are more prevalent and harder to prevent. Obviously, it's up to you though to select the socks that fit your shoes, budget, and type of training and hiking you do.

The illustration shows slip-on spikes on the trail running shoes. This photo was taken while preparing for a winter snow trail run in the Rocky Mountains at 10,000' in February. I wear or carry spikes like this whenever I expect there to be snow or ice on the trails. In the higher sections of Colorado it could be any day of the year, but in general, between the Fourth of July and Labor Day you should not need them. Of course, pay attention to the weather and know before you go. For most summer ascents they are not required.

Photo, next page is one of my favorite cold weather shoe and sock combinations, from top, toe socks, loop cushion mountaineering socks, trail running shoes with slip-on spikes.

Summit Success

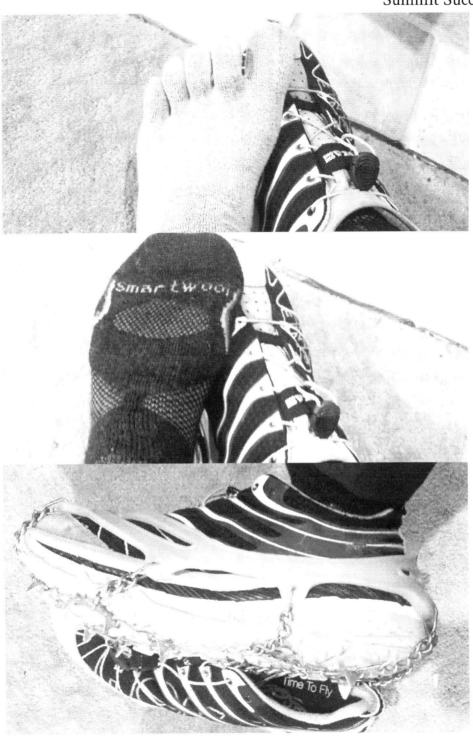

Beware of waterproof materials. There are several ways to make leather and fabric waterproof, including waterproof-breathable membranes lining the boot. There are two common ways to do this. One is to line the boot outer shell with the layered membrane. In this way stitching penetrates the barrier and unless the manufacturer took the extra step of applying an adhesive strip or tape over the seam, it will leak unless you apply a seam sealer, sold at most outdoor shops. You will have to reapply it on a regular basis.

The second way to line the boot with a membrane is to insert a sock style full boot liner of the barrier material. It is usually more expensive to do this, and it can bunch up at the toes and at the welt where the insole rests against the edges of the boot. You should seal the top and around the tongue where it is sewn in, if needed.

Most waterproof-breathable membranes are actually not as miraculous as the marketing would have you believe. If you fill your boot with water it will stay inside the boot until you take it off and drain it. Do not let water run over the top or sides of the tongue. Many people feel they also have less ventilation than other types of fabric or leather boots. In hot weather this can be a real annoyance to deal with.

Clothing

You want to carry and wear the least amount of clothing you can get away with, yet remain safe for upcoming weather events. In the peak of the summer in the Rockies it might be around 40 at the trailhead in the early morning, then maybe 60 on the summit at Noon, then around 80 back at the trailhead in the early afternoon. It might also rain, and if it's a bit colder that day, snow near the summit. You'll need to be able to function within a range of comfort in those activity and climate zones.

I like to wear synthetic trekking pants with zippers at the knee to convert them into shorts. Remember to apply sunscreen to your lower legs if you're going to do this. Some companies use a thinner airy weave and others a rougher rugged weave. It's up to you which you prefer. Some people don't like the feel of sweat on water and wind resistant thin soft-shell type fabric. You probably don't need anything that thick for a Lower 48 Summer hike.

For underwear, there are several synthetic options, from panties to briefs to boxer briefs to boxers. Whatever you like can be found in a quick wicking synthetic blend. Remember that cotton can feel pretty miserable when you sweat and it bunches up between your legs. Maybe you don't feel that, and you can experiment during training to find out your own preference.

On top, I like to wear a synthetic t-shirt as my bottom layer. If it's cold in the morning or at the summit I can put a thin fleece shirt or jacket over it. I've had better success with the more textured feeling polyesters than the shiny sleek ones. Lycra and nylon blends tend to hold water and feel chilled when a cloud creeps over the sun. You'll see a lot of fancy names for materials that are supposed to stay stink-free when you sweat. Some people have sweat that naturally reacts with the material and causes it to smell horrible, no matter what their personal hygiene or laundry soap. I use a Febreze blend laundry detergent on my running clothes and it seems to work pretty good for me.

I take a thin insulated puffy vest or jacket, depending on the weather forecast. I've been taking a thin vest most of the time in the last few summers. I've used it quite a few times and been satisfied to accept being a bit cold now and then. The thin insulated jackets are quite popular and almost every serious outdoor clothing manufacturer makes one. If rain is a possibility I prefer synthetic over down, and the modern synthetics are really light and compress well enough that it's almost irrelevant as an excuse to go with down.

My rainwear is meant only for a few hours at most, again depending on the forecast. I like a thin light cycling rain jacket, but if it's going to be a downpour I will take a waterproof membrane parka, though the lightest one I can get away with. Though a waterproof membrane jacket is not so breathable that you won't feel any plastic baggy effect, it works in a pinch as a wind jacket too.

If I am confident that I'll only get a mild shower, a water and wind resistant jacket with no membrane is really light and compresses to almost nothing. I suggest though that unless you are a really experienced hiker willing to accept the consequences of ending up in a downpour with only a wind jacket, take the membrane jacket. Be safe until you're experienced enough to make an informed decision you can live with.

Gloves could be thin light fleece or soft-shell gloves with gripping pads on the fingers and palms. If it's going to really rain, you might consider gloves with a thin membrane shell. Some people have circulation or other problems that lead to really cold hands. Toss a couple hand warmers in soft-shell fleece gloves and you should be fine. Obviously be smart. If you know you need full on ski or insulated gloves, stick them in the pack and be prepared. I almost always wear cycling gloves with padded panels for my trekking poles. I wear them when I am trail running without poles too so that my palms and knuckles are protected in case I take a fall on rough terrain. I've used them like that several times. If I'm climbing a 14er wearing them then I carry a thin pair of wind gloves to put over them if it's chilly out.

Baseball or other sun caps are essential to keep the sun out of your eyes and off your face. It's also good at keeping rain off your glasses or sunglasses. I have a couple of running synthetic ball style brimmed caps. Some brims are stiff and some soft. Some brims are long and some are short. Sometimes I just grab one and go. If you're going to be going up really steep terrain though a long brim can get in the way of your uphill vision. Be warned. I have friends who swear by the cycling style billed caps of thin synthetic material. Lots of people hike in fishing caps. It's whatever you have that you like.

A beanie cap can help if it's really chilly. Try it on over or under your baseball cap if you want to keep the sun and rain off your face with this combination on. I also like to wear a Buff, a thin tube of material that can be formed into a cap or neck and face cover. It's pretty versatile and can even take the place of a beanie. Look at the package for ideas on how to use it several ways. Some people also like to wear bandanas wrapped around their neck, head or over the top of their head. If you're training outside on trails you'll probably see pretty much everything by the time you get out on your dream hike.

Sunglasses are so essential that I'm putting them in this section with clothing. You want the whole nine yards with the sunglasses. Protect your eyes. If you'll be on snow you'll want more protection from reflected light. If you have contacts, you'll be able to wear just about anything, but if you're going to wear prescription sunglasses you'll need the darkest ones you can get. BUT! If you take off from the trailhead in the dark, you'll need to see, and the sunglasses won't help much seeing in the dark. You might be stuck taking your sunglasses in a case and switching them out when the sun rises. I was stuck out after dark in prescription sunglasses once. I ended up taking them off and hiking out by headlamp with very blurry vision. Fortunately the

Summit Success

trail was wide, obvious and safe enough. You could also check into the various self-adjusting prescription sunglasses.

Photos on the next couple pages show clothing. First photo is baseball and beanie caps, gloves, buff and an insulated vest. Second photo is an insulated vest, a fleece jacket, and a wind/rain jacket.

Training for Hiking, Mountaineering, and Peak Bagging – by Charles Miske

Summit Success

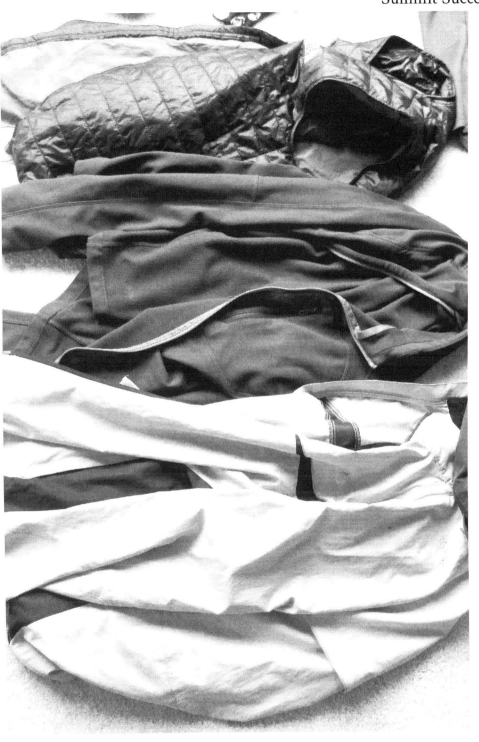

Training for Hiking, Mountaineering, and Peak Bagging – by Charles Miske

Snacks and Water

Believe it or not, snacking and drinking on the trail will be among the most important factors in the success of your adventure. I'm going to start in reverse order, with water. I say water because I mean water. Not juice. Not sports drinks. I mean water. In general, use water whenever possible. If you do choose to use some type of electrolyte mix, use the tablets or powder and try it at half strength. In my experience hiking, trekking, trail running and cycling, I've found that I myself hydrate a lot better at half strength for most electrolyte mixes. To establish your needs, try it during training and see how it works for you. Remember that at altitude many things can change, including how your body processes liquids and electrolytes.

That being said, other than failing on your adventure, in general, there should be no long term affects from having too much or too little chemicals in your water for one single solitary day hike.

As far as snacks are concerned, a common practice is to hike for 50 to 55 minutes, sit for 5 to 10 minutes and continue in one hour chunks of time. You can adjust this a bit to suit the terrain. If there is a really beautiful place for photos or just watching the scenery, and you're within 10 minutes or so of your intended stopping time, great, just do it. If you're on a steep section with no convenient place to stop, continue on to the top and stop there. It's not rocket science.

I mentioned previously that you should have about nine 200 calorie snacks. Six for on the way up, and maybe three for on the way down. That should work out to be a decent number if you want to do it that way.

Everything you bring as a snack should be compact, easy to open and eat, and easy to digest. You need to save your garbage and pack it all out, including pull tabs, zip strips, caps, and other tiny little things you might just let blow away under other circumstances. Remember the Leave No Trace principles I mentioned earlier. Leave it in better condition than you found it if possible. At least don't contribute to more unsightly waste.

Something you might not be aware of is that as you go up in altitude your body processes food slightly differently and sends subtle signals about that to your brain to affect your appetite. Things you might adore and enjoy at home will seem disgusting to you at altitude. I've had the pleasure of experiencing this for myself on several foreign expeditions, and through friends I've taken on mountaineering trips who suddenly found out that the 10 pounds of food they brought along for base camp at 14,000' is almost useless and unpalatable. Be prepared.

Some of my own tried and true, tested on myself favorites include:
- Fruit snacks
- Foil pouch screw top fruit puree

- Vanilla wafers
- Graham crackers
- Bel vita cookies
- Fig-style fruit bars
- Chocolate bars
- Salted almonds
- Chewy granola and cereal bars

If you're wanting to go all "endurance athlete" on this one, then you can try:
- Goo packets (Hammer is my favorite)
- Honey Stinger Waffles
- Jelly Belly Sport Beans

There are a slew of these available at any running, hiking, or other sports store. If I'm in a hurry these work great, and I use them in my longer trail runs, so I'm used to digesting them on the go.

Going old-school, a lot of people like:
- Jerky
- Foil pouches of salmon or sardines
- Trail mix with nuts and raisins
- M&M's, Skittles, etc.
- Gummy Bears
- Coated pretzels

Remember that whatever you take must be full of energy and keep you going. Some people like to have a shot or two of caffeine and you can get that in some of the sports goo packets and other sports products. Some people bring along a small plastic bottle of cola, sports drink, or even a little can or bottle of espresso. If you need it, those are some ideas, and I'm sure you can go from there to decide what would work best for you. Be sure to pack out your empties of whatever you choose to take with.

Something else I need to point out is that now is not the time to start losing fat. You don't want to cut your energy input so far below your output that you bonk and crash and can't do your big hike. Eat and drink during your hike. Lose fat in training. It's tough to wrap your head around this if you've been in fat burning mode for very long.

Photo, next page, is an assortment of goodies I keep on hand to fuel my own hiking adventures. Graham crackers, vanilla wafers, Bel-Vita crackers, dark chocolate and other things as in the previous lists.

Miscellaneous Gear

You will most likely want a set of trekking poles. You will probably use them the whole way, so they number of sections and folded or collapsed size doesn't matter too much right now. You could even use an old pair of ski poles. If you live near a ski area, when the snow melts out these will be all over under the lift towers. To size them, hold your arm bent at the elbow, forearm parallel to the ground, and the pole grip in your hand. The tip should be touching an area between the ground and the top of your shoe.

If your pole is adjustable and you are on a steep uphill slope, then you might make it a bit shorter, 3" or so, and if you're going downhill on a steep slope, perhaps a bit longer, again, 3-4" should be sufficient.

Of course, you'll need water containers of some sort. Most people seem to sweat a bit more at altitude, so need a bit more water than they anticipate. Over the years I've found that 2-3 liters will do the job for most normal people so long as you are in good shape, and can adjust your clothing to reduce needless sweating. If you know that you will need more, than try to anticipate that, but remember that water weighs a bit more than 2 pounds per liter. Carrying 10 pounds of water up a steep slope is not pleasant. Fortunately, it's one of those things that gets lighter as you go higher.

There are several different types of containers. You could just buy three one-liter plastic disposable water bottles and stick those in your pack. Be sure to smash them and carry them out for recycling when empty though. The classic Nalgene bottles are quite common on the trails. Cycling and running bottles are also common. I like collapsible plastic bottles, similar to the bladders. Some people like the metal Sigg bottles, but they are a bit heavier than some of the plastic alternatives, and you can't see what's inside to plan and monitor your water rations for the day.

Photo, next page, is an assortment of water bottles typically used for hiking and other physical activities. Just about anything that won't leak will do the job.

Summit Success

You should have a headlamp for just in case. You never know when you'll end up out in the dark, and a headlamp can save your life as you hike out, or even for signaling if you're stuck. There are many different brands and styles. I like a 2-way LED headlamp that takes a few AAA batteries. They don't weigh much, and have a High and Low beam option to save batteries. Most of these have a battery life of dozens of hours, more than a whole night of use. Put a pair of brand new Alkaline or Lithium batteries in and don't use it until you need it other than to take a hike or two in the dark to test it out. If you're camping near the trail then a spare set of AAA batteries is really small and light. That way you can use the headlamp in camp and in the tent and still feel safe in the event of an emergency.

If you want to carry a small flashlight instead, there are also several models of AA or AAA hand flashlights with adjustable beams. I much prefer to have the light turn with my head keeping my hands free to use my trekking poles or for support on rocks and trees, especially on steep and rugged terrain. In an emergency though you can make do if it's a matter of life and death.

You should have some toilet paper or similar. Take what you think you would normally need for a day, plus a little bit more, and roll it up neatly inside a zip lock baggie. You might also consider bringing along a baggie to put the used ones in so you don't leave paper behind to blow in the wind. Produce bags work well, but the best are the doggie doo bags. You can get these at many stores now, including grocery stores, but a lot of parks have some in a dispenser along the walking paths too. Many mountains now require you to use a container for human waste, including Rainier, Denali, and Aconcagua. It makes a lot of sense in high use areas.

A camera is almost essential. You'll need to do the classic summit selfies. Pictures of marmots and goats are always fun to share with friends and relatives. Your phone might be sufficient, or you might want to use a better one, with better zoom capability. You don't need to go all out and take a large DSLR, unless it's your hobby and you really want to. There are several small waterproof shockproof freeze proof cameras out there now, in case you want to go all out on this.

Alternatively, a few high zoom cameras in a very small lightweight format are now on the market for reasonable prices. You'll have to protect them from water and keep them warm enough, but they are worth that small hassle for the fantastic photos. A good accessory to take is a little flexible tripod that you can form over rocks and branches to take distant selfies with your shutter timer. Be sure your battery is all charged up in your camera before you go.

Photo, next page, shows an assortment of gear as mentioned in this chapter, including Purificup Water Purifier, matches, lighter, GPS, altimeter watch, charging cable, outdoor camera, Goal Zero charger, flashlight accessory, headlamp, bear bell.

Training for Hiking, Mountaineering, and Peak Bagging – by Charles Miske

Summit Success

An altimeter watch is fun, and makes a great summit shot with the elevation visible on it. Be sure to calibrate it and know how to use it. Don't waste time away from your adventure because you can't figure out how to make it work. A compass is great, if you know how to use it, otherwise it's almost useless. It works best with a topographical map of your area. You can print these up yourself from software and the Net, or buy them. A GPS is also a great option, again, if you know how to use it. In any case, there are no guarantees that any of these will work or be beneficial, so be psychologically prepared to accept their failure and deal with it accordingly.

Some people like music, some don't. It's controversial either way. If you're going with music, please don't carry a huge boom box on your shoulder like a caricature from the 80's and let everyone on the trail share your tastes. Use a small player, or your phone, in a pocket somewhere, possibly in a weatherproof case or even zip lock bag, with ear buds. Wear only one. With one ear exposed you can hear other hikers, dogs, wild animals and trail hazards and react appropriately to them. Tuck the other one under a strap or rubber band it to the cord to keep it from flopping around. Even so, keep the volume down low enough that you can hear and think. Enjoy what you can. That being said, if you're a no music kind of person, then let them be and accept that some people like to hike to music. It's all good.

If you like being prepared for anything, then a battery pack recharger might be in order. Currently I use a Switch 8 from Goal Zero. It's light, easy to recharge via USB and has a small flashlight head attachment in case you want to make use of the battery pack. If charging your phone, camera, headlamp, GPS, or whatever is on the list of requirements for this, then be sure to take the appropriate cables with to plug it in.

You could also take a small emergency water purifier. I've used the Purificup water filter with great success, all around the world, including the Caucasus of Russia and Andes in Argentina and on the Carstensz trek in Indonesia. Some people like the UV purifiers, or straw type purifiers. If you think you might drink more than you're carrying and need more, and there is water on the trail, you might consider it.

If you have contacts and need solution, or a medical condition requiring regular use of medicine or injections, be sure to keep those handy enough for the type of use you require. Additionally, a small first aid kit could be helpful, especially a blister kit including some moleskin, liquid skin, Band-Aids, antibiotic ointment, and a few disinfectant pads in individual use foil packets. Put it in a zip lock bag for simplicity. If you're training in your trail boots or shoes, this shouldn't be a major issue with big surprises on the trail. It's for just in case. Be sure to have some sunscreen and lip balm very handy to refresh them often. High altitude sun has less filtering from the atmosphere and can burn deceptively fast.

A pocket knife is pretty old school and to be honest, in thousands of hikes over my life I've used it maybe a handful of times, primarily to trim a cracked fingernail. I've never used a Leatherman tool on a hike and for my own use, relegate it to car camping or expeditions, where it might come in handy to clean a clogged stove, though many of the better stoves come apart by hand.

A bear bell is essential when hiking in bear country, as you'll find in Montana, but can be a lot of fun jingling down the trail in any case.

Photo, next page, shows a very small simple first aid kit that will fit into a small zip lock baggie.

Summit Success

Training for Hiking, Mountaineering, and Peak Bagging – by Charles Miske

The Twelve Week Program Overview:

This is the Main Training Cycle. The plan in a nutshell is build your cardio endurance for walking uphill. I have set weekly goals based on vertical feet per hour more than any other criterion. I plan the progression similar to training for a 5K or 10K run. I want you to get in vertical feet of training every week, but not so much in one day that you can't recover in time for the next session. I also don't want you to train over the number of vertical feet you'll need to do for your graduation – a Colorado 14er or other large mountain.

In a running training progression you try to make an increase of only 10% per week in your weekly mileage. This seems to work good for them, so I'll recommend that to you. Since you'll be doing about 3-4000' of vertical at the end of the program – your target last week of training in this program – I worked it backwards to create each week's target goal. I haven't really addressed miles yet so far. Most of the 14ers you're likely to do as a first are between 3 and 6 miles one way. Some are a bit longer or shorter based on your vehicle since some trailheads are safe for 4x4 access only and other vehicles will have to park down the road a bit. Of course, you can sometimes get a ride with someone who has a gnarlier vehicle too.

If you're doing a cardio machine workout on anything other than a treadmill you might run into a problem with not getting enough miles in. The Stepmill runs at about 99% inclination so you only go approximately the same distance as height. 3600 vertical feet is about 3600 linear feet – less than a mile. Otherwise, with a treadmill you'll definitely get the miles in. If you're training outside by walking your problem will most likely be in getting the vertical in. Unless you happen to live near a large steep hill. Or near a stadium or other stair climbing facility. You will definitely have to keep vertical feet in the front of your mind as you train.

As a general principle I want you to do three to four sessions of cardio each week. Some people can do four and thrive on it, but I want you to allow yourself plenty of time to recover between each training session so monitor your own progress and recovery and make it work for you. In the beginning of your Adjustment Cycle you started with only 20:00 minutes for each workout, but now you should be at 50:00. We're going to start this next Cycle at 60:00. By the end of the 12 week program these workout sessions will be extended to between 90:00 and 120:00 minutes. That's 2 hours. Please allow yourself the time to do this. It's a serious major undertaking for many people, and well worth it to your self-esteem and sense of accomplishment.

If you pay careful attention to the charts I'm about to show you first, with the big picture, you'll see that you could get away with some really intense half hour sessions and still hit your goals. At least in the first several weeks. At the end though you will really need to be hitting the cardio at an hour or two per session to make it work. Unless you're really fast and strong in your endurance.

I also want you to continue to do two sessions of strength training each week. Again, allow yourself plenty of time to recover. We started in the Adjustment Cycle with a session length of about an hour. We're going to stick with that now for the rest of the program. Before long you'll be doing so much time training cardio that you'll appreciate the shorter days spent on strength training.

I don't think it's really a good idea for a total beginner to train at a harder level than what I give for each week. If you're coming into this as an experienced trainer you might jump in at a middle point somewhere and then since I've explained the math to you, create your own goals from whatever point you're coming into this.

First of all, I'm going to show you the basic outline of the concept behind the plan, with a little bit of math thrown in. That's all just in case you're a really OCD kind of person and want to put together your own daily goals and plans based on the math and you enjoy that kind of thing.

To be totally honest with you, some of my best 5-star reviews for my other training, fitness, and nutrition manuals are from really OCD people who really enjoy doing their own math and I just point the way out to them and give them subtle nudges along the path to success. This works for them. Awesomely.

If that is totally not you, then skip ahead to the weekly goal training sections and let me do some of your thinking for you then.

Chart 1: Vertical Goals using a Treadmill

Week	Target Vertical	Target Miles	Miles at 3%	Miles at 6%	Miles at 12%	Miles at 15%
5	1,130	5.26	7.13	3.57	1.78	1.43
6	1,255	5.78	7.92	3.96	1.98	1.58
7	1,395	6.36	8.81	4.40	2.20	1.76
8	1,550	7.00	9.78	4.89	2.45	1.96
9	1,722	7.70	10.87	5.44	2.72	2.17
10	1,913	8.47	12.08	6.04	3.02	2.42
11	2,126	9.31	13.42	6.71	3.36	2.68
12	2,362	10.25	14.91	7.46	3.73	2.98
13	2,624	11.27	16.57	8.28	4.14	3.31
14	2,916	12.40	18.41	9.20	4.60	3.68
15	3,240	13.64	20.45	10.23	5.11	4.09
16	3,600	15.00	22.73	11.36	5.68	4.55

In the above chart the twelve weeks of the Main Training Cycle are laid out with the target weekly vertical feet in column 2, and your target total miles in column 3. The next four columns show how many miles you will need to walk at 3%, 6%, 12% and 15% to achieve that goal.

I want to make this "easy" on you without laying down a set of exact numbers and goals and targets to micromanage your progress. I want you to take some responsibility for your own training. I'm providing a reasonable progression for you to adjust to your own ability and time.

The huge exception comes in near the end of the program. Notice that in order to get in 3,600' at 3% you'd have to go for over 22 miles a week. That's 7.5 miles per training day! If you are able to run at a pace of 8:00 for an hour, you could do it pretty quickly. But if you're like the rest of us, it ain't going to happen like that.

At 12% you would only have to average a little less than 2 miles per day. If you can go at our goal speed of 1.5 mph this is less than 90 minutes of cardio per training day. I hope that makes sense and works for you. I have to say though that I do want you to spend as much time as possible at 15% if your treadmill will allow you to, and you can achieve that level of strength endurance, but it's all there in the chart for you to make work for yourself.

Summit Success

If you did the whole Adjustment Training Cycle, then you were up to 9% at the end of it. You could break the next 16 weeks into four 4-week cycles. Spend the first cycle working up to 12% and the next cycle working up to 15%. From there, if you don't have access to an Incline Treadmill, you could mix in some box stepping or Stepmill training to get in some more steep terrain simulation. Otherwise, you'll be fine doing much of your training at 15%.

An idea for the last few weeks is to do 5 miles on your treadmill set at 15% split over two workouts, then do the other two workouts at 3% to get in another 9-10 miles of total training for a weekly average closer to 15 miles. If you're doing 15 mile weeks, you'll be awesome on the mountain. It's fine though if you can get in at least 10 miles in each training week as you get closer to your hike.

In the next chart, I'm showing the training goals that you would strive to achieve if you have access to an Incline Treadmill. One of the more common Incline Treadmills has a preset button for 16, 24, 32, and 40 percent inclination. If yours doesn't then it should only take a second to type in the inclination you choose to train at. My own recommendation is that you break the training program into six 4-week cycles, with a cycle spent at each maximum inclination. So spend a month at 16%, a month at 24% etc. until you're spending a month at 40%.

Keep in mind that 40% is pretty steep, and your mileage goals will need to be made up with some more shallow training. If you have the mind for it, you could spend two or three training sessions at 40% or another steep inclination, then make up your miles with one or two long sessions at a shallower angle that you can maintain 3.0+MPH on.

Chart 2: Vertical Goals for Incline Treadmill

Week	Target Vertical	Target Miles	Miles at 16%	Miles at 24%	Miles at 32%	Miles at 40%
5	1,130	5.26	1.34	0.89	0.67	0.53
6	1,255	5.78	1.49	0.99	0.74	0.59
7	1,395	6.36	1.65	1.10	0.83	0.66
8	1,550	7.00	1.83	1.22	0.92	0.73
9	1,722	7.70	2.04	1.36	1.02	0.82
10	1,913	8.47	2.26	1.51	1.13	0.91
11	2,126	9.31	2.52	1.68	1.26	1.01
12	2,362	10.25	2.80	1.86	1.40	1.12
13	2,624	11.27	3.11	2.07	1.55	1.24
14	2,916	12.40	3.45	2.30	1.73	1.38
15	3,240	13.64	3.84	2.56	1.92	1.53
16	3,600	15.00	4.26	2.84	2.13	1.70

Everything I stated in the previous section on the treadmill applies, except it's very easy to get in your vertical with the Incline Treadmill set steeply and you can then make up your mileage goals on flatter terrain outside or at a lower inclination.

Chart 3: Vertical Goals using a Stairmaster Stepmill

Training Week	Target Vertical	Target Miles	Minutes at 25 SPM	Minutes at 30 SPM	Minutes at 35 SPM	Minutes at 40 SPM
5	1,255	5.26	75.31	62.76	53.80	47.07
6	1,395	5.78	83.68	69.74	59.77	52.30
7	1,550	6.36	92.98	77.48	66.41	58.11
8	1,722	7.00	103.31	86.09	73.79	64.57
9	1,913	7.70	114.79	95.66	81.99	71.74
10	2,126	8.47	127.55	106.29	91.10	79.72
11	2,362	9.31	141.72	118.10	101.23	88.57
12	2,624	10.25	157.46	131.22	112.47	98.42
13	2,916	11.27	174.96	145.80	124.97	109.35
14	3,240	12.40	194.40	162.00	138.86	121.50
15	3,600	13.64	216.00	180.00	154.29	135.00
16	4,000	15.00	240.00	200.00	171.43	150.00

In this above chart, I show the same weeks and target vertical. This time I show four speeds on a Stairmaster Stepmill. 25 steps per minute, 30 steps per minute, 35 steps per minute, and 40 steps per minute. I only took this chart as low as 25 SPM because that's where you should have been during your Adjustment Training Cycle. If you need to go more slowly than that, you can use my Stepmill Calculator to help figure out how many feet you do per hour and go from there. Since the "Miles" reporting feature on the Stairmaster is obviously flawed and completely wrong (sorry folks) I am using minutes as your goal on this chart.

Going to Week One again for the math:

824 feet at 25 steps per minute = 49.41 minutes

49.41 minutes ÷ 3 training days = 16.47 minutes

So you'd be doing 3 sessions of 17 minutes each at 25 steps per minute. Sounds easy, right? Well that's up to you. Even at the end of the program, at week 16 you have three 90 minute sessions at 20 steps per minute to achieve your goal for that week.

Keep in mind, one of my favorite phrases here, that you are not getting any miles in at all. Well, only a few. You'll have to get in your mileage goals doing something else. It is pretty good to get in all your vertical in one session if you can, which is much easier on a Stepmill than it is on a treadmill, especially if it isn't an Incline Treadmill. It's much more specific to your upcoming mountain climb if you can do one 4000' training session.

In my Week One example above, that's one 50:00 session on the Stepmill, with two or three other sessions to get in your miles. If you want to combine things, this might be the easiest way of all. One day in the gym for your Stepmill workout, and three days walking outside for miles is a great way to get the best of both types of training. I have to admit, it's one of my own personal favorites.

Chart 4: Vertical Goals for Box Stepping and Stairs

Training Week	Target Vertical	Target Miles	Steps at 9"	Steps at 12"	Steps at 15"	Steps at 18"
5	1,255	5.26	1674	1255	1004	837
6	1,395	5.78	1860	1395	1116	930
7	1,550	6.36	2066	1550	1240	1033
8	1,722	7.00	2296	1722	1377	1148
9	1,913	7.70	2551	1913	1531	1275
10	2,126	8.47	2834	2126	1701	1417
11	2,362	9.31	3149	2362	1890	1575
12	2,624	10.25	3499	2624	2100	1750
13	2,916	11.27	3888	2916	2333	1944
14	3,240	12.40	4320	3240	2592	2160
15	3,600	13.64	4800	3600	2880	2400
16	4,000	15.00	5333	4000	3200	2667

For those of you who are using real stairs or box stepping to get in your vertical, I'm including the above chart. For simplicity I'm showing how many steps total equal your vertical weekly goal for a few common sizes of step. I mentioned steps and boxes before. If you measure the step where you are able to train, and it's within an inch of the 9" step in the chart, it should be good enough, and if it's 8", that's 1/9th less, or 11%. If you just add 10% to the weekly step goals that is plenty close enough. I hope that makes sense.

I think an 18" step is the largest that most normal trainers can use for timed stepping so this chart doesn't go beyond that. Even more advanced trainers could have trouble consistently hitting the step goals at 18".

Let's do a quick example to show how to calculate your box stepping session goals, again, from Week One. Assume we measured our stairs in our apartment building and they are 9" vertical rise, with 11 steps per landing. I'm trying to make this simple, as you'll see in the math below:

Week One Example using Stairs:

1098 steps ÷ 11 steps per landing = 100 landings

Training for Hiking, Mountaineering, and Peak Bagging – by Charles Miske

100 landings ÷ 4 training sessions = 25 landings per training session

I hope that was simple enough. I hope your own circumstance is as simple, but the math is there for you to use.

If you have a particular time goal in mind, it's a bit more complicated. In the Week One Example above, you might want to do a training session in 25:00 (again with the simple math) which means that you have one minute or 1:00 per landing. That might seem a bit on the slow side though. Here's a big Gotcha!

If your apartment building does not have 25 consecutive landings, you will have to descend every so many landings. Descending does not count as ascending and is not part of your vertical goal achievement. Surprise! So you will have to hit your landings and return to the start and do laps of your stairways until you have achieved your daily training goal.

There is a huge plus side to this, and that is that you are also training the descent. Going down the stairs uses the muscles associated with going downhill on the mountain. These are the eccentric muscles that usually take a huge beating on the descent from the summit. Several dozen people have asked how to train them, and this is the secret. Go up and down stairs for vertical goals.

You can't train this on a normal treadmill or Stepmill. There is an Incline Treadmill that goes into negative inclination, up to negative 6%, or downhill 6%. It feels odd to train on one, and I have. I like to run/walk intervals on it, and the way you have to keep your leg muscles flexed to prevent pounding the deck is tough, but is excellent training for the downhill motion of hiking.

If you're going to use a box, you will get your eccentric, or downhill training, on every step. You count a step as every time your shoulders come up over the box with your legs and hips "straightened" but don't exaggerate the motion, please. One advantage to this is that you can set a metronome app with an intended pace that is more difficult to achieve on stairs. Stairs have landings, often with turns, that prevent adhering strictly to the ticking of a metronome.

Usually, you face the box, step up with one foot, bring the other foot up beside it and straighten. You return to the beginning by reversing the motion and then repeat. Be very careful that you don't bang your legs on the edges of the box. If you don't have an official box you could possibly get away with using a stair, a park bench, a picnic table. Just make sure it's going to hold your weight under dynamic force. You could be applying 300 pounds or more of multi-directional pressure in the middle of a step. You do not want to be flipping a picnic table over on yourself. Just saying.

The metronome app I've experimented with allows me to set a pace, say 40 beats per minute, then give an alternate alert tone every 10 beats, or steps as I'm using it. The setting for that is *Beats-per-Bar*. I can also set it to alert me with another tone for the in-between steps called *Clicks-per-Beat*. UP, up, down, down, UP, up, down, down, UP, up, down, down….

If I set a goal to take 250 steps that day, I can just listen for the big alert tone 25 times. Unless my heart rate is out of this world, I can manage to keep that level of awareness for that amount of time.

Week One Example Using 12" Box:

824 steps ÷ 2 training sessions = 412 steps per training session

412 steps ÷ 30 steps per minute = 13.74 minutes

412 steps ÷ 12 step chunks = 34.3 chunks

For training over your target, if you're using a metronome as I would be, then you just have to listen to the big beat 35 times and you're done. Just keep your feet moving to the beat and it'll be a fantastic workout. If you want more info on my metronome app settings, in the above example it would be set for:
- 40 Beats per Minute
- 12 Beats per Measure
- 4 Clicks per Beat

Since we're getting this done in just a few minutes, you have plenty of time to do some walking or running to get in your miles during other training sessions. Box stepping, stair stepping, Stepmill training are all very efficient at getting in vertical. If you can, make the effort to get some in every week.

Other Cardio Machines:

The Cybex Arc Trainer, NordicTrack FreeStrider, and a few other elliptical style machines have the ability to be set to a more "vertical" operation. These two report vertical feet as well as miles. While I think the numbers reported are somewhat accurate enough, I also feel that they aren't the same as using a treadmill or stepmill. Neither one allows you to bear 100% of your own weight. If you train on these machines almost exclusively you will be surprised to feel how heavy your legs feel on the day you attempt your 14er.

I think these machines can be incorporated into this training program, but I think they should be where you get any additional miles or feet in. I use the one I have access to for my warm-up before doing weight training. I do record the vertical feet in my own training journal, but don't count it toward any weekly goals.

The Remainder of the Sixteen Weeks

If you're interested in just getting out and doing it now, and don't want to read a lot, here's the section for you. It's a very simple breakdown based on charts that will get you to the end of the sixteen weeks in really good shape. It's based on quite simple math and is basically split into both 3 and 4 exactly identical cardio training sessions per week. Remember that in between you've got to get in 2 weight or strength training sessions. Those aren't in the charts, but you can make it work just by putting them on the calendar.

Now is the time to be putting weights in the backpack. These are on every chart, but are the same on every chart. I could have put them all in a different single chart, but thought it would be better for you to have them on every chart.

There are some really good things about it, and some really bad things about it. First the good.

Since every training session is exactly identical, it's easier to mix and match and put together a cross training style program. Pick a Day One, a Day Two, a Day Three, and if your own schedule allows, a Day Four from any chart and at the end of the week you've met your goals.

If you're doing cross-training warm-ups with your strength training, like riding an elliptical, cycle, or rowing machine, then you'll do the workouts without the deduction for the 10:00 – 12:00 warm-up and cool-down walking. If you are going to use walking or jogging for your strength training warm-up and cool-down then use the charts with the deduction for the extra 2 miles each week. That's assuming that you can do a half mile in 10:00 – 12:00 (ten to twelve minutes). That's a fairly brisk (for some) 2.5-3.0 MPH. You can also say that's a 20:00 – 24:00 pace for those who use a GPS watch. In the big scheme of things it doesn't matter whether that walk is inside or out, so long as it's not steep. Save that for your cardio training days.

How to use the charts to follow:

I'll show some examples here of the various charts I'm providing for you to get your training inspiration and guidance from. I hope that by taking it apart like this it will make perfect sense and be simple to incorporate into your own training program. I'll start first with the Incline Treadmill. Then I'll show the Stepmill.

16% - 4x per Week - no Mileage Deduction for Strength Training

Week	5
Target Weekly Vertical Ft	1,130
Target Weekly Miles	5.26
Weekly Miles at 16%	1.337
Incline Miles Per Session (x4)	0.334
Weekly Miles Deficit	3.920
Warm-up/Cool-down Each per session	0.490
Backpack Weight	2

This is for an Incline Treadmill set to 16% for your Weekly Vertical Training.

At the top "5" is the week of training you are currently engaged in.

Below that "1,130" is your target vertical feet for the week.

Then "5.26" is the target mileage for the week.

In row 4 is "1.337" which is the number of miles for the week you would walk on the treadmill at 16% inclination to get in your vertical target.

In row 5 is "0.334" which is the number of miles you would go during each of four training sessions at your 16% inclination. All other miles would be flat, or 0%.

The Miles Deficit is what you get when you subtract your inclined miles from your mileage goal. In this case it's "3.920" so in the row below that you see that you'd have to walk "0.490" miles as both a warm-up and a cool-down before and after each inclined training session. That should then be (Mile Deficit / 8) which means you're making up the deficit with 4 warm-ups and 4 cool-downs. One each before and after every cardio training session.

The "no Deduction" charts imply that you're doing cross-training like cycling or elliptical as your warm-up and cool-down for your strength training.

Finally we have the total weight of your backpack. Many inexpensive backpacks will weigh in around 2 pounds empty, so that's a good starting point.

16% - 3x per Week - Mileage Deduction for Strength Training

Week	5
Target Weekly Vertical Ft	1,130
Target Weekly Miles	5.26
Weekly Miles at 16%	1.337
Incline Miles Per Session (x3)	0.446
Weekly Strength Training Miles	2.000
Weekly Miles Deficit	1.920
Warm-up/Cool-down Each per session	0.320
Backpack Weight	2

Again, for the Incline Treadmill set to 16% but we're only doing three days of cardio training and we are doing walking/running/jogging for our strength training warm-up and cool-down.

This chart has a couple of minor differences from the previous example. Row 4 is the Incline Miles per training session assuming only 3 cardio training sessions in a week.

The row below that, 5, shows the Weekly Miles done by walking or running or jogging for your strength training warm-up and cool-down. You'll be doing 2 strength training sessions every week, and if you do a 0.5 mile warm-up walk and a 0.5 mile cool-down walk every time, that will take 2.0 miles off of your weekly mileage goal.

That impacts the Warm-up/Cool-down miles per cardio training session quite a bit and could save a lot of time on your cardio training days. This is especially good for saving time when you consider that you have to do something for your warm-up and cool-down on your strength training days anyway.

4x per Week - no Mileage Deduction for Strength Training

This is for a Stairmaster Stepmill with 4 cardio training sessions per week and no additional miles from strength training warm-up and cool-down.

Training Week	5
Target Vertical	1,255
Target Miles	5.26
Steps	1883
Weekly Hours at 30 SPM	1:02
Minutes each for 4 training sessions	0:15
Steps per Training Session	471
Week Miles from Stepmill	0.27
Week Miles Deficit	4.99
Warm-up & Cool-down miles ea. per session	0.62
Backpack Weight	2

A Stepmill typically is controlled by entering a steps-per-minute pace. In this case that's 30 Steps per Minute. By measuring the steps I've calculated the horizontal and vertical feet you'd be moving in those minutes.

So in this case you'd have to be on the Stepmill at 30 SPM for 15:00 (fifteen minutes) for each of the 4 training sessions that week. The Steps per Training Session "471" is really only there in case you'll be using this chart for 8" stair or box training and isn't really relevant to you on the Stepmill. See how low that Week Miles from Stepmill "0.27" is like a really low number. Yeah. At 9" of forward motion per step 471 steps doesn't add up to much very quickly.

Otherwise it's the same as the others.

9" - 3x per Week - Mileage Deduction for Strength Training

Training Week	5
Target Vertical	1,255
Target Miles	5.26
Steps	1674
Weekly Hours at 30 SPM	0:55
Minutes each for 3 training sessions	0:13
Steps per Training Session	419
Week Miles from Stairs	0.24
Weekly Strength Training Miles	2.000
Week Miles Deficit	3.02
Warm-up & Cool-down miles ea. per session	0.38
Backpack Weight	2

Finally we have an example from Stair Climbing on 9" stairs. It's similar to the chart for the Stepmill, but 9" is roughly 13% larger than 8" even though it doesn't sound like a lot. Here though see how your Steps per Training Session "419" is appreciably lower than the previous example at 471 steps.

You can use this for Box Stepping as well. Remember how previously I explained how to set a metronome and count your laps for both stairs and boxes so that you can get in your steps at a decent pace. The taller the step or box the more difficult it will be to maintain that 30 SPM pace.

If you're really strong and fast you can do an 18" box or skip steps, but I do recommend against trying hard to go too fast that big of a leap in case you hurt yourself. You've been warned to the possibility.

Treadmill Training for Remaining Twelve Weeks

The treadmill is now set at 15% after your Adjustment Cycle and these charts assume 3 or 4 identical workouts per week to achieve your weekly goals. One of the benefits of this is that you can more easily mix it up by picking a workout off of each of these charts four times a week and know you're achieving the goals for that week. Do not mix and match between the 3 and 4 session per week charts as it will not work in accomplishing your weekly goals. Also do not mix and match between charts for the mileage deduction for the warm-up and cool-down miles for strength training.

First we'll look at 4x per Week - no Mileage Deduction for Strength Training. Then we'll look at 3x per Week - no Mileage Deduction for Strength Training. Following that is 4x per Week - Mileage Deduction for Strength Training. Lastly is 3x per Week - Mileage Deduction for Strength Training.

4x per Week - no Mileage Deduction for Strength Training

Weeks 5-8

Week	5	6	7	8
Target Weekly Vertical Ft	1,130	1,255	1,395	1,550
Target Weekly Miles	5.26	5.78	6.36	7.00
Weekly Miles at 15%	1.426	1.585	1.761	1.957
Incline Miles Per Session (4 sessions/week)	0.357	0.396	0.440	0.489
Weekly Miles Deficit	3.831	4.198	4.600	5.041
Warm-up/Cool-down Each per session	0.479	0.525	0.575	0.630
Backpack Weight	2	3	4	5

Weeks 9-12

Week	9	10	11	12
Target Weekly Vertical Ft	1,722	1,913	2,126	2,362
Target Weekly Miles	7.70	8.47	9.31	10.25
Weekly Miles at 15%	2.174	2.416	2.684	2.982
Incline Miles Per Session (4 sessions/week)	0.544	0.604	0.671	0.746
Weekly Miles Deficit	5.523	6.051	6.630	7.263
Warm-up/Cool-down Each per session	0.690	0.756	0.829	0.908
Backpack Weight	6	7	8	9

Weeks 13-16

Week	13	14	15	16
Target Weekly Vertical Ft	2,624	2,916	3,240	3,600
Target Weekly Miles	11.27	12.40	13.64	15.00
Weekly Miles at 15%	3.314	3.682	4.091	4.545
Incline Miles Per Session (4 sessions/week)	0.828	0.920	1.023	1.136
Weekly Miles Deficit	7.956	8.715	9.545	10.455
Warm-up/Cool-down Each per session	0.995	1.089	1.193	1.307
Backpack Weight	10	11	12	13

Remember that this is for 4 Cardio Training Sessions per Week with Cross-Training for Strength Training Warm-Up and Cool-Down.

3x per Week - no Mileage Deduction for Strength Training

Weeks 5-8

Week	5	6	7	8
Target Weekly Vertical Ft	1,130	1,255	1,395	1,550
Target Weekly Miles	5.26	5.78	6.36	7.00
Weekly Miles at 15%	1.426	1.585	1.761	1.957
Incline Miles Per Session (x3)	0.475	0.528	0.587	0.652
Weekly Miles Deficit	3.831	4.198	4.600	5.041
Warm-up/Cool-down Each per session	0.638	0.700	0.767	0.840
Backpack Weight	2	3	4	5

Weeks 9-12

Week	9	10	11	12
Target Weekly Vertical Ft	1,722	1,913	2,126	2,362
Target Weekly Miles	7.70	8.47	9.31	10.25
Weekly Miles at 15%	2.174	2.416	2.684	2.982
Incline Miles Per Session (x3)	0.725	0.805	0.895	0.994
Weekly Miles Deficit	5.523	6.051	6.630	7.263
Warm-up/Cool-down Each per session	0.921	1.009	1.105	1.210
Backpack Weight	6	7	8	9

Weeks 13-16

Week	13	14	15	16
Target Weekly Vertical Ft	2,624	2,916	3,240	3,600
Target Weekly Miles	11.27	12.40	13.64	15.00
Weekly Miles at 15%	3.314	3.682	4.091	4.545
Incline Miles Per Session (x3)	1.105	1.227	1.364	1.515
Weekly Miles Deficit	7.956	8.715	9.545	10.455
Warm-up/Cool-down Each per session	1.326	1.452	1.591	1.742
Backpack Weight	10	11	12	13

Remember that this is for 3 Cardio Training Sessions per Week with Cross-Training for Strength Training Warm-Up and Cool-Down.

4x per Week - Mileage Deduction for Strength Training

Weeks 5-8

Week	5	6	7	8
Target Weekly Vertical Ft	1,130	1,255	1,395	1,550
Target Weekly Miles	5.26	5.78	6.36	7.00
Weekly Miles at 15%	1.426	1.585	1.761	1.957
Incline Miles Per Session (4 sessions/week)	0.357	0.396	0.440	0.489
Weekly Strength Training Miles	2.000	2.000	2.000	2.000
Weekly Miles Deficit	1.831	2.198	2.600	3.041
Warm-up/Cool-down Each per session	0.229	0.275	0.325	0.380
Backpack Weight	2	3	4	5

Weeks 9-12

Week	9	10	11	12
Target Weekly Vertical Ft	1,722	1,913	2,126	2,362
Target Weekly Miles	7.70	8.47	9.31	10.25
Weekly Miles at 15%	2.174	2.416	2.684	2.982
Incline Miles Per Session (4 sessions/week)	0.544	0.604	0.671	0.746
Weekly Strength Training Miles	2.000	2.000	2.000	2.000
Weekly Miles Deficit	3.523	4.051	4.630	5.263
Warm-up/Cool-down Each per session	0.440	0.506	0.579	0.658
Backpack Weight	6	7	8	9

Weeks 13-16

Week	13	14	15	16
Target Weekly Vertical Ft	2,624	2,916	3,240	3,600
Target Weekly Miles	11.27	12.40	13.64	15.00
Weekly Miles at 15%	3.314	3.682	4.091	4.545
Incline Miles Per Session (4 sessions/week)	0.828	0.920	1.023	1.136
Weekly Strength Training Miles	2.000	2.000	2.000	2.000
Weekly Miles Deficit	5.956	6.715	7.545	8.455
Warm-up/Cool-down Each per session	0.745	0.839	0.943	1.057
Backpack Weight	10	11	12	13

Remember that this is for 4 Cardio Training Sessions per Week and walking/jogging/running for Strength Training Warm-Up and Cool-Down.

3x per Week - Mileage Deduction for Strength Training

Weeks 5-8

Week	5	6	7	8
Target Weekly Vertical Ft	1,130	1,255	1,395	1,550
Target Weekly Miles	5.26	5.78	6.36	7.00
Weekly Miles at 15%	1.426	1.585	1.761	1.957
Incline Miles Per Session (x3)	0.475	0.528	0.587	0.652
Weekly Strength Training Miles	2.000	2.000	2.000	2.000
Weekly Miles Deficit	1.831	2.198	2.600	3.041
Warm-up/Cool-down Each per session	0.305	0.366	0.433	0.507
Backpack Weight	2	3	4	5

Weeks 9-12

Week	9	10	11	12
Target Weekly Vertical Ft	1,722	1,913	2,126	2,362
Target Weekly Miles	7.70	8.47	9.31	10.25
Weekly Miles at 15%	2.174	2.416	2.684	2.982
Incline Miles Per Session (x3)	0.725	0.805	0.895	0.994
Weekly Strength Training Miles	2.000	2.000	2.000	2.000
Weekly Miles Deficit	3.523	4.051	4.630	5.263
Warm-up/Cool-down Each per session	0.587	0.675	0.772	0.877
Backpack Weight	6	7	8	9

Training for Hiking, Mountaineering, and Peak Bagging – by Charles Miske

Weeks 13-16

Week	13	14	15	16
Target Weekly Vertical Ft	2,624	2,916	3,240	3,600
Target Weekly Miles	11.27	12.40	13.64	15.00
Weekly Miles at 15%	3.314	3.682	4.091	4.545
Incline Miles Per Session (x3)	1.105	1.227	1.364	1.515
Weekly Strength Training Miles	2.000	2.000	2.000	2.000
Weekly Miles Deficit	5.956	6.715	7.545	8.455
Warm-up/Cool-down Each per session	0.993	1.119	1.258	1.409
Backpack Weight	10	11	12	13

Remember that this is for 3 Cardio Training Sessions per Week and walking/jogging/running for Strength Training Warm-Up and Cool-Down.

Incline Treadmill Training for Remaining Twelve Weeks

The Incline Treadmill is pretty much the same as the treadmill, only we can go a bit steeper if we like. I'm going to post the charts for 16%, 20%, and 24%. Since this is essentially a beginner program I don't think there's that much value right now in doing anything beyond 24%. If you want to get charts for more inclination than that please ask on my http://sevensummits-body.com/summitsuccess page and I'll see what we can do for you.

One recommendation I have is that you could start with 4 weeks at 16%. Move on to 4 weeks at 20%. Then finish with 4 weeks at 24%. That would make a great progressive resistance style of training that will most likely put you at your peak just as it's time for the summit of your peak. Yeah, I know. Anyway, it's a great way to go that extra bit of effort.

Otherwise, it would be fine to do 6 weeks at 16% and then another 6 at 20%. Like I stated before, mixing and matching between workouts is fine, so long as you stay within the day count. So you can mix up any from the "3 sessions per week" charts. You can mix up any from the "4 sessions per week" charts. Don't mix it up between those two day count groupings though. That prevents you from achieving your mileage and vertical goals. You might go over or under, and it would be a mess to sort through. You've been warned.

16% - 4x per Week - no Mileage Deduction for Strength Training

Weeks 5-8

Week	5	6	7	8
Target Weekly Vertical Ft	1,130	1,255	1,395	1,550
Target Weekly Miles	5.26	5.78	6.36	7.00
Weekly Miles at 16%	1.337	1.486	1.651	1.834
Incline Miles Per Session (x4)	0.334	0.371	0.413	0.459
Weekly Miles Deficit	3.920	4.297	4.711	5.163
Warm-up/Cool-down Each per session	0.490	0.537	0.589	0.645
Backpack Weight	2	3	4	5

Weeks 9-12

Week	9	10	11	12
Target Weekly Vertical Ft	1,722	1,913	2,126	2,362
Target Weekly Miles	7.70	8.47	9.31	10.25
Weekly Miles at 16%	2.038	2.265	2.516	2.796
Incline Miles Per Session (x4)	0.510	0.566	0.629	0.699
Weekly Miles Deficit	5.659	6.202	6.798	7.449
Warm-up/Cool-down Each per session	0.707	0.775	0.850	0.931
Backpack Weight	6	7	8	9

Weeks 13-16

Week	13	14	15	16
Target Weekly Vertical Ft	2,624	2,916	3,240	3,600
Target Weekly Miles	11.27	12.40	13.64	15.00
Weekly Miles at 16%	3.107	3.452	3.835	4.261
Incline Miles Per Session (x4)	0.777	0.863	0.959	1.065
Weekly Miles Deficit	8.163	8.945	9.801	10.739
Warm-up/Cool-down Each per session	1.020	1.118	1.225	1.342
Backpack Weight	10	11	12	13

Remember that this is for 4 Cardio Training Sessions per Week with Cross-Training for Strength Training Warm-Up and Cool-Down.

16% - 3x per Week - no Mileage Deduction for Strength Training

Weeks 5-8

Week	5	6	7	8
Target Weekly Vertical Ft	1,130	1,255	1,395	1,550
Target Weekly Miles	5.26	5.78	6.36	7.00
Weekly Miles at 16%	1.337	1.486	1.651	1.834
Incline Miles Per Session (x3)	0.446	0.495	0.550	0.611
Weekly Miles Deficit	3.920	4.297	4.711	5.163
Warm-up/Cool-down Each per session	0.653	0.716	0.785	0.861
Backpack Weight	2	3	4	5

Weeks 9-12

Week	9	10	11	12
Target Weekly Vertical Ft	1,722	1,913	2,126	2,362
Target Weekly Miles	7.70	8.47	9.31	10.25
Weekly Miles at 16%	2.038	2.265	2.516	2.796
Incline Miles Per Session (x3)	0.679	0.755	0.839	0.932
Weekly Miles Deficit	5.659	6.202	6.798	7.449
Warm-up/Cool-down Each per session	0.943	1.034	1.133	1.242
Backpack Weight	6	7	8	9

Weeks 13-16

Week	13	14	15	16
Target Weekly Vertical Ft	2,624	2,916	3,240	3,600
Target Weekly Miles	11.27	12.40	13.64	15.00
Weekly Miles at 16%	3.107	3.452	3.835	4.261
Incline Miles Per Session (x3)	1.036	1.151	1.278	1.420
Weekly Miles Deficit	8.163	8.945	9.801	10.739
Warm-up/Cool-down Each per session	1.361	1.491	1.634	1.790
Backpack Weight	10	11	12	13

Remember that this is for 3 Cardio Training Sessions per Week with Cross-Training for Strength Training Warm-Up and Cool-Down.

16% - 4x per Week - Mileage Deduction for Strength Training

Weeks 5-8

Week	5	6	7	8
Target Weekly Vertical Ft	1,130	1,255	1,395	1,550
Target Weekly Miles	5.26	5.78	6.36	7.00
Weekly Miles at 16%	1.337	1.486	1.651	1.834
Incline Miles Per Session (x3)	0.446	0.495	0.550	0.611
Weekly Miles Deficit	3.920	4.297	4.711	5.163
Warm-up/Cool-down Each per session	0.653	0.716	0.785	0.861
Backpack Weight	2	3	4	5

Weeks 9-12

Week	9	10	11	12
Target Weekly Vertical Ft	1,722	1,913	2,126	2,362
Target Weekly Miles	7.70	8.47	9.31	10.25
Weekly Miles at 16%	2.038	2.265	2.516	2.796
Incline Miles Per Session (x3)	0.679	0.755	0.839	0.932
Weekly Miles Deficit	5.659	6.202	6.798	7.449
Warm-up/Cool-down Each per session	0.943	1.034	1.133	1.242
Backpack Weight	6	7	8	9

Weeks 13-16

Week	13	14	15	16
Target Weekly Vertical Ft	2,624	2,916	3,240	3,600
Target Weekly Miles	11.27	12.40	13.64	15.00
Weekly Miles at 16%	3.107	3.452	3.835	4.261
Incline Miles Per Session (x3)	1.036	1.151	1.278	1.420
Weekly Miles Deficit	8.163	8.945	9.801	10.739
Warm-up/Cool-down Each per session	1.361	1.491	1.634	1.790
Backpack Weight	10	11	12	13

Remember that this is for 4 Cardio Training Sessions per Week and walking/jogging/running for Strength Training Warm-Up and Cool-Down.

16% - 3x per Week - Mileage Deduction for Strength Training

Weeks 5-8

Week	5	6	7	8
Target Weekly Vertical Ft	1,130	1,255	1,395	1,550
Target Weekly Miles	5.26	5.78	6.36	7.00
Weekly Miles at 16%	1.337	1.486	1.651	1.834
Incline Miles Per Session (x3)	0.446	0.495	0.550	0.611
Weekly Strength Training Miles	2.000	2.000	2.000	2.000
Weekly Miles Deficit	1.920	2.297	2.711	3.163
Warm-up/Cool-down Each per session	0.320	0.383	0.452	0.527
Backpack Weight	2	3	4	5

Weeks 9-12

Week	9	10	11	12
Target Weekly Vertical Ft	1,722	1,913	2,126	2,362
Target Weekly Miles	7.70	8.47	9.31	10.25
Weekly Miles at 16%	2.038	2.265	2.516	2.796
Incline Miles Per Session (x3)	0.679	0.755	0.839	0.932
Weekly Strength Training Miles	2.000	2.000	2.000	2.000
Weekly Miles Deficit	3.659	4.202	4.798	5.449
Warm-up/Cool-down Each per session	0.610	0.700	0.800	0.908
Backpack Weight	6	7	8	9

Weeks 13-16

Week	13	14	15	16
Target Weekly Vertical Ft	2,624	2,916	3,240	3,600
Target Weekly Miles	11.27	12.40	13.64	15.00
Weekly Miles at 16%	3.107	3.452	3.835	4.261
Incline Miles Per Session (x3)	1.036	1.151	1.278	1.420
Weekly Strength Training Miles	2.000	2.000	2.000	2.000
Weekly Miles Deficit	6.163	6.945	7.801	8.739
Warm-up/Cool-down Each per session	1.027	1.157	1.300	1.456
Backpack Weight	10	11	12	13

Remember that this is for 3 Cardio Training Sessions per Week and walking/jogging/running for Strength Training Warm-Up and Cool-Down.

20% - 4x per Week - no Mileage Deduction for Strength Training

Weeks 5-8

Week	5	6	7	8
Target Weekly Vertical Ft	1,130	1,255	1,395	1,550
Target Weekly Miles	5.26	5.78	6.36	7.00
Weekly Miles at 20%	1.070	1.189	1.321	1.468
Incline Miles Per Session (x4)	0.267	0.297	0.330	0.367
Weekly Miles Deficit	4.188	4.594	5.041	5.530
Warm-up/Cool-down Each per session	0.523	0.574	0.630	0.691
Backpack Weight	2	3	4	5

Weeks 9-12

Week	9	10	11	12
Target Weekly Vertical Ft	1,722	1,913	2,126	2,362
Target Weekly Miles	7.70	8.47	9.31	10.25
Weekly Miles at 20%	1.631	1.812	2.013	2.237
Incline Miles Per Session (x4)	0.408	0.453	0.503	0.559
Weekly Miles Deficit	6.067	6.655	7.301	8.008
Warm-up/Cool-down Each per session	0.758	0.832	0.913	1.001
Backpack Weight	6	7	8	9

Weeks 13-16

Week	13	14	15	16
Target Weekly Vertical Ft	2,624	2,916	3,240	3,600
Target Weekly Miles	11.27	12.40	13.64	15.00
Weekly Miles at 20%	2.485	2.761	3.068	3.409
Incline Miles Per Session (x4)	0.621	0.690	0.767	0.852
Weekly Miles Deficit	8.784	9.635	10.568	11.591
Warm-up/Cool-down Each per session	1.098	1.204	1.321	1.449
Backpack Weight	10	11	12	13

Remember that this is for 4 Cardio Training Sessions per Week with Cross-Training for Strength Training Warm-Up and Cool-Down.

20% - 3x per Week - no Mileage Deduction for Strength Training

Weeks 5-8

Week	5	6	7	8
Target Weekly Vertical Ft	1,130	1,255	1,395	1,550
Target Weekly Miles	5.26	5.78	6.36	7.00
Weekly Miles at 20%	1.070	1.189	1.321	1.468
Incline Miles Per Session (x3)	0.357	0.396	0.440	0.489
Weekly Miles Deficit	4.188	4.594	5.041	5.530
Warm-up/Cool-down Each per session	0.698	0.766	0.840	0.922
Backpack Weight	2	3	4	5

Weeks 9-12

Week	9	10	11	12
Target Weekly Vertical Ft	1,722	1,913	2,126	2,362
Target Weekly Miles	7.70	8.47	9.31	10.25
Weekly Miles at 20%	1.631	1.812	2.013	2.237
Incline Miles Per Session (x3)	0.544	0.604	0.671	0.746
Weekly Miles Deficit	6.067	6.655	7.301	8.008
Warm-up/Cool-down Each per session	1.011	1.109	1.217	1.335
Backpack Weight	6	7	8	9

Weeks 13-16

Week	13	14	15	16
Target Weekly Vertical Ft	2,624	2,916	3,240	3,600
Target Weekly Miles	11.27	12.40	13.64	15.00
Weekly Miles at 20%	2.485	2.761	3.068	3.409
Incline Miles Per Session (x3)	0.828	0.920	1.023	1.136
Weekly Miles Deficit	8.784	9.635	10.568	11.591
Warm-up/Cool-down Each per session	1.464	1.606	1.761	1.932
Backpack Weight	10	11	12	13

Remember that this is for 3 Cardio Training Sessions per Week with Cross-Training for Strength Training Warm-Up and Cool-Down.

20% - 4x per Week - Mileage Deduction for Strength Training

Weeks 5-8

Week	5	6	7	8
Target Weekly Vertical Ft	1,130	1,255	1,395	1,550
Target Weekly Miles	5.26	5.78	6.36	7.00
Weekly Miles at 20%	1.070	1.189	1.321	1.468
Incline Miles Per Session (x4)	0.267	0.297	0.330	0.367
Weekly Strength Training Miles	2.000	2.000	2.000	2.000
Weekly Miles Deficit	2.188	2.594	3.041	3.530
Warm-up/Cool-down Each per session	0.273	0.324	0.380	0.441
Backpack Weight	2	3	4	5

Weeks 9-12

Week	9	10	11	12
Target Weekly Vertical Ft	1,722	1,913	2,126	2,362
Target Weekly Miles	7.70	8.47	9.31	10.25
Weekly Miles at 20%	1.631	1.812	2.013	2.237
Incline Miles Per Session (x4)	0.408	0.453	0.503	0.559
Weekly Strength Training Miles	2.000	2.000	2.000	2.000
Weekly Miles Deficit	4.067	4.655	5.301	6.008
Warm-up/Cool-down Each per session	0.508	0.582	0.663	0.751
Backpack Weight	6	7	8	9

Weeks 13-16

Week	13	14	15	16
Target Weekly Vertical Ft	2,624	2,916	3,240	3,600
Target Weekly Miles	11.27	12.40	13.64	15.00
Weekly Miles at 20%	2.485	2.761	3.068	3.409
Incline Miles Per Session (x4)	0.621	0.690	0.767	0.852
Weekly Strength Training Miles	2.000	2.000	2.000	2.000
Weekly Miles Deficit	6.784	7.635	8.568	9.591
Warm-up/Cool-down Each per session	0.848	0.954	1.071	1.199
Backpack Weight	10	11	12	13

Remember that this is for 4 Cardio Training Sessions per Week and walking/jogging/running for Strength Training Warm-Up and Cool-Down.

20% - 3x per Week - Mileage Deduction for Strength Training

Weeks 5-8

Week	5	6	7	8
Target Weekly Vertical Ft	1,130	1,255	1,395	1,550
Target Weekly Miles	5.26	5.78	6.36	7.00
Weekly Miles at 20%	1.070	1.189	1.321	1.468
Incline Miles Per Session (x3)	0.357	0.396	0.440	0.489
Weekly Strength Training Miles	2.000	2.000	2.000	2.000
Weekly Miles Deficit	2.188	2.594	3.041	3.530
Warm-up/Cool-down Each per session	0.365	0.432	0.507	0.588
Backpack Weight	2	3	4	5

Weeks 9-12

Week	9	10	11	12
Target Weekly Vertical Ft	1,722	1,913	2,126	2,362
Target Weekly Miles	7.70	8.47	9.31	10.25
Weekly Miles at 20%	1.631	1.812	2.013	2.237
Incline Miles Per Session (x3)	0.544	0.604	0.671	0.746
Weekly Strength Training Miles	2.000	2.000	2.000	2.000
Weekly Miles Deficit	4.067	4.655	5.301	6.008
Warm-up/Cool-down Each per session	0.678	0.776	0.883	1.001
Backpack Weight	6	7	8	9

Weeks 13-16

Week	13	14	15	16
Target Weekly Vertical Ft	2,624	2,916	3,240	3,600
Target Weekly Miles	11.27	12.40	13.64	15.00
Weekly Miles at 20%	2.485	2.761	3.068	3.409
Incline Miles Per Session (x3)	0.828	0.920	1.023	1.136
Weekly Strength Training Miles	2.000	2.000	2.000	2.000
Weekly Miles Deficit	6.784	7.635	8.568	9.591
Warm-up/Cool-down Each per session	1.131	1.273	1.428	1.598
Backpack Weight	10	11	12	13

Remember that this is for 3 Cardio Training Sessions per Week and walking/jogging/running for Strength Training Warm-Up and Cool-Down.

24% - 4x per Week - no Mileage Deduction for Strength Training

Weeks 5-8

Week	5	6	7	8
Target Weekly Vertical Ft	1,130	1,255	1,395	1,550
Target Weekly Miles	5.26	5.78	6.36	7.00
Weekly Miles at 24%	0.892	0.991	1.101	1.223
Incline Miles Per Session (x4)	0.223	0.248	0.275	0.306
Weekly Miles Deficit	4.366	4.793	5.261	5.775
Warm-up/Cool-down Each per session	0.546	0.599	0.658	0.722
Backpack Weight	2	3	4	5

Weeks 9-12

Week	9	10	11	12
Target Weekly Vertical Ft	1,722	1,913	2,126	2,362
Target Weekly Miles	7.70	8.47	9.31	10.25
Weekly Miles at 24%	1.359	1.510	1.678	1.864
Incline Miles Per Session (x4)	0.340	0.377	0.419	0.466
Weekly Miles Deficit	6.339	6.957	7.636	8.381
Warm-up/Cool-down Each per session	0.792	0.870	0.955	1.048
Backpack Weight	6	7	8	9

Weeks 13-16

Week	13	14	15	16
Target Weekly Vertical Ft	2,624	2,916	3,240	3,600
Target Weekly Miles	11.27	12.40	13.64	15.00
Weekly Miles at 24%	2.071	2.301	2.557	2.841
Incline Miles Per Session (x4)	0.518	0.575	0.639	0.710
Weekly Miles Deficit	9.199	10.096	11.080	12.159
Warm-up/Cool-down Each per session	1.150	1.262	1.385	1.520
Backpack Weight	10	11	12	13

Remember that this is for 4 Cardio Training Sessions per Week with Cross-Training for Strength Training Warm-Up and Cool-Down.

24% - 3x per Week - no Mileage Deduction for Strength Training

Weeks 5-8

Week	5	6	7	8
Target Weekly Vertical Ft	1,130	1,255	1,395	1,550
Target Weekly Miles	5.26	5.78	6.36	7.00
Weekly Miles at 24%	0.892	0.991	1.101	1.223
Incline Miles Per Session (x3)	0.297	0.330	0.367	0.408
Weekly Miles Deficit	4.366	4.793	5.261	5.775
Warm-up/Cool-down Each per session	0.728	0.799	0.877	0.962
Backpack Weight	2	3	4	5

Weeks 9-12

Week	9	10	11	12
Target Weekly Vertical Ft	1,722	1,913	2,126	2,362
Target Weekly Miles	7.70	8.47	9.31	10.25
Weekly Miles at 24%	1.359	1.510	1.678	1.864
Incline Miles Per Session (x3)	0.453	0.503	0.559	0.621
Weekly Miles Deficit	6.339	6.957	7.636	8.381
Warm-up/Cool-down Each per session	1.056	1.160	1.273	1.397
Backpack Weight	6	7	8	9

Weeks 13-16

Week	13	14	15	16
Target Weekly Vertical Ft	2,624	2,916	3,240	3,600
Target Weekly Miles	11.27	12.40	13.64	15.00
Weekly Miles at 24%	2.071	2.301	2.557	2.841
Incline Miles Per Session (x3)	0.690	0.767	0.852	0.947
Weekly Miles Deficit	9.199	10.096	11.080	12.159
Warm-up/Cool-down Each per session	1.533	1.683	1.847	2.027
Backpack Weight	10	11	12	13

Remember that this is for 3 Cardio Training Sessions per Week with Cross-Training for Strength Training Warm-Up and Cool-Down.

24% - 4x per Week - Mileage Deduction for Strength Training

Weeks 5-8

Week	5	6	7	8
Target Weekly Vertical Ft	1,130	1,255	1,395	1,550
Target Weekly Miles	5.26	5.78	6.36	7.00
Weekly Miles at 24%	0.892	0.991	1.101	1.223
Incline Miles Per Session (x4)	0.223	0.248	0.275	0.306
Weekly Strength Training Miles	2.000	2.000	2.000	2.000
Weekly Miles Deficit	2.366	2.793	3.261	3.775
Warm-up/Cool-down Each per session	0.296	0.349	0.408	0.472
Backpack Weight	2	3	4	5

Weeks 9-12

Week	9	10	11	12
Target Weekly Vertical Ft	1,722	1,913	2,126	2,362
Target Weekly Miles	7.70	8.47	9.31	10.25
Weekly Miles at 24%	1.359	1.510	1.678	1.864
Incline Miles Per Session (x4)	0.340	0.377	0.419	0.466
Weekly Strength Training Miles	2.000	2.000	2.000	2.000
Weekly Miles Deficit	4.339	4.957	5.636	6.381
Warm-up/Cool-down Each per session	0.542	0.620	0.705	0.798
Backpack Weight	6	7	8	9

Weeks 13-16

Week	13	14	15	16
Target Weekly Vertical Ft	2,624	2,916	3,240	3,600
Target Weekly Miles	11.27	12.40	13.64	15.00
Weekly Miles at 24%	2.071	2.301	2.557	2.841
Incline Miles Per Session (x4)	0.518	0.575	0.639	0.710
Weekly Strength Training Miles	2.000	2.000	2.000	2.000
Weekly Miles Deficit	7.199	8.096	9.080	10.159
Warm-up/Cool-down Each per session	0.900	1.012	1.135	1.270
Backpack Weight	10	11	12	13

Remember that this is for 4 Cardio Training Sessions per Week and walking/jogging/running for Strength Training Warm-Up and Cool-Down.

24% - 3x per Week - Mileage Deduction for Strength Training

Weeks 5-8

Week	5	6	7	8
Target Weekly Vertical Ft	1,130	1,255	1,395	1,550
Target Weekly Miles	5.26	5.78	6.36	7.00
Weekly Miles at 24%	0.892	0.991	1.101	1.223
Incline Miles Per Session (x3)	0.297	0.330	0.367	0.408
Weekly Strength Training Miles	2.000	2.000	2.000	2.000
Weekly Miles Deficit	2.366	2.793	3.261	3.775
Warm-up/Cool-down Each per session	0.394	0.465	0.543	0.629
Backpack Weight	2	3	4	5

Weeks 9-12

Week	9	10	11	12
Target Weekly Vertical Ft	1,722	1,913	2,126	2,362
Target Weekly Miles	7.70	8.47	9.31	10.25
Weekly Miles at 24%	1.359	1.510	1.678	1.864
Incline Miles Per Session (x3)	0.453	0.503	0.559	0.621
Weekly Strength Training Miles	2.000	2.000	2.000	2.000
Weekly Miles Deficit	4.339	4.957	5.636	6.381
Warm-up/Cool-down Each per session	0.723	0.826	0.939	1.064
Backpack Weight	6	7	8	9

Weeks 13-16

Week	13	14	15	16
Target Weekly Vertical Ft	2,624	2,916	3,240	3,600
Target Weekly Miles	11.27	12.40	13.64	15.00
Weekly Miles at 24%	2.071	2.301	2.557	2.841
Incline Miles Per Session (x3)	0.690	0.767	0.852	0.947
Weekly Strength Training Miles	2.000	2.000	2.000	2.000
Weekly Miles Deficit	7.199	8.096	9.080	10.159
Warm-up/Cool-down Each per session	1.200	1.349	1.513	1.693
Backpack Weight	10	11	12	13

Remember that this is for 3 Cardio Training Sessions per Week and walking/jogging/running for Strength Training Warm-Up and Cool-Down.

Training for Hiking, Mountaineering, and Peak Bagging – by Charles Miske

Stepmill Training for Remaining Twelve Weeks

The Stepmill training sessions are in the chart on the following page.

Note that the Warm-up and Cool-down Miles column shows the amount of flat walking or running that you would have to do both before and after the Stepmill workout for that day.

As an example, in the first row for Week 5 you see that it states .60 miles. That means that you will walk or run .60 miles, then do the requisite 15.69 minutes (from the spreadsheet math, here rounded to 15:00) on the Stepmill, then do another .60 miles on a relatively flat surface, like a treadmill set to 0% inclination and call it a day.

Note that the time values are automatically rounded, so there will be a few seconds missing here and there. Notice for Week 5 (from the chart for 4x per Week - no Mileage Deduction) as an example, 1:02 hours total, comprised of four sessions of 15:00 or a total loss of thirty seconds per training session.

Do not mix and match between the 3 and 4 session per week charts as it will not work in accomplishing your weekly goals. Also do not mix and match between charts for the mileage deduction for the warm-up and cool-down miles for strength training.

First we'll look at 4x per Week - no Mileage Deduction for Strength Training. Then we'll look at 3x per Week - no Mileage Deduction for Strength Training. Following that is 4x per Week - Mileage Deduction for Strength Training. Lastly is 3x per Week - Mileage Deduction for Strength Training.

4x per Week - no Mileage Deduction for Strength Training

Weeks 5-8

Training Week	5	6	7	8
Target Vertical	1,255	1,395	1,550	1,722
Target Miles	5.26	5.78	6.36	7.00
Steps	1883	2092	2325	2583
Weekly Hours at 30 SPM	1:02	1:09	1:17	1:26
Minutes each for 4 training sessions	0:15	0:17	0:19	0:21
Steps per Training Session	471	524	582	646
Week Miles from Stepmill	0.27	0.30	0.33	0.37
Week Miles Deficit	4.99	5.49	6.03	6.63
Warm-up & Cool-down miles ea. per session	0.62	0.69	0.75	0.83
Backpack Weight	2	3	4	5

Weeks 9-12

Training Week	9	10	11	12
Target Vertical	1,913	2,126	2,362	2,624
Target Miles	7.70	8.47	9.31	10.25
Steps	2870	3189	3543	3937
Weekly Hours at 30 SPM	1:35	1:46	1:58	2:11
Minutes each for 4 training sessions	0:23	0:26	0:29	0:32
Steps per Training Session	718	798	886	985
Week Miles from Stepmill	0.41	0.45	0.50	0.56
Week Miles Deficit	7.29	8.01	8.81	9.69
Warm-up & Cool-down miles ea. per session	0.91	1.00	1.10	1.21
Backpack Weight	6	7	8	9

Weeks 13-16

Training Week	13	14	15	16
Target Vertical	2,916	3,240	3,600	4,000
Target Miles	11.27	12.40	13.64	15.00
Steps	4374	4860	5400	6000
Weekly Hours at 30 SPM	2:25	2:42	3:00	3:20
Minutes each for 4 training sessions	0:36	0:40	0:45	0:50
Steps per Training Session	1094	1215	1350	1500
Week Miles from Stepmill	0.62	0.69	0.77	0.85
Week Miles Deficit	10.65	11.71	12.87	14.15
Warm-up & Cool-down miles ea. per session	1.33	1.46	1.61	1.77
Backpack Weight	10	11	12	13

Remember that this is for 4 Cardio Training Sessions per Week with Cross-Training for Strength Training Warm-Up and Cool-Down.

3x per Week - no Mileage Deduction for Strength Training

Weeks 5-8

Training Week	5	6	7	8
Target Vertical	1,255	1,395	1,550	1,722
Target Miles	5.26	5.78	6.36	7.00
Steps	1883	2092	2325	2583
Weekly Hours at 30 SPM	1:02	1:09	1:17	1:26
Minutes each for 3 training sessions	0:20	0:23	0:25	0:28
Steps per Training Session	628	698	775	861
Week Miles from Stepmill	0.27	0.30	0.33	0.37
Week Miles Deficit	4.99	5.49	6.03	6.63
Warm-up & Cool-down miles ea. per session	0.83	0.91	1.01	1.11
Backpack Weight	2	3	4	5

Weeks 9-12

Training Week	9	10	11	12
Target Vertical	1,913	2,126	2,362	2,624
Target Miles	7.70	8.47	9.31	10.25
Steps	2870	3189	3543	3937
Weekly Hours at 30 SPM	1:35	1:46	1:58	2:11
Minutes each for 3 training sessions	0:31	0:35	0:39	0:43
Steps per Training Session	957	1063	1181	1313
Week Miles from Stepmill	0.41	0.45	0.50	0.56
Week Miles Deficit	7.29	8.01	8.81	9.69
Warm-up & Cool-down miles ea. per session	1.21	1.34	1.47	1.61
Backpack Weight	6	7	8	9

Weeks 13-16

Training Week	13	14	15	16
Target Vertical	2,916	3,240	3,600	4,000
Target Miles	11.27	12.40	13.64	15.00
Steps	4374	4860	5400	6000
Weekly Hours at 30 SPM	2:25	2:42	3:00	3:20
Minutes each for 3 training sessions	0:48	0:54	1:00	1:06
Steps per Training Session	1458	1620	1800	2000
Week Miles from Stepmill	0.62	0.69	0.77	0.85
Week Miles Deficit	10.65	11.71	12.87	14.15
Warm-up & Cool-down miles ea. per session	1.77	1.95	2.14	2.36
Backpack Weight	10	11	12	13

Remember that this is for 3 Cardio Training Sessions per Week with Cross-Training for Strength Training Warm-Up and Cool-Down.

4x per Week - Mileage Deduction for Strength Training

Weeks 5-8

Training Week	5	6	7	8
Target Vertical	1,255	1,395	1,550	1,722
Target Miles	5.26	5.78	6.36	7.00
Steps	1883	2092	2325	2583
Weekly Hours at 30 SPM	1:02	1:09	1:17	1:26
Minutes each for 4 training sessions	0:15	0:17	0:19	0:21
Steps per Training Session	471	524	582	646
Week Miles from Stepmill	0.27	0.30	0.33	0.37
Weekly Strength Training Miles	2.000	2.000	2.000	2.000
Week Miles Deficit	2.99	5.49	6.03	6.63
Warm-up & Cool-down miles ea. per session	0.37	0.69	0.75	0.83
Backpack Weight	2	3	4	5

Weeks 9-12

Training Week	9	10	11	12
Target Vertical	1,913	2,126	2,362	2,624
Target Miles	7.70	8.47	9.31	10.25
Steps	2870	3189	3543	3937
Weekly Hours at 30 SPM	1:35	1:46	1:58	2:11
Minutes each for 4 training sessions	0:23	0:26	0:29	0:32
Steps per Training Session	718	798	886	985
Week Miles from Stepmill	0.41	0.45	0.50	0.56
Weekly Strength Training Miles	2.000	2.000	2.000	2.000
Week Miles Deficit	7.29	8.01	8.81	9.69
Warm-up & Cool-down miles ea. per session	0.91	1.00	1.10	1.21
Backpack Weight	6	7	8	9

Weeks 13-16

Training Week	13	14	15	16
Target Vertical	2,916	3,240	3,600	4,000
Target Miles	11.27	12.40	13.64	15.00
Steps	4374	4860	5400	6000
Weekly Hours at 30 SPM	2:25	2:42	3:00	3:20
Minutes each for 4 training sessions	0:36	0:40	0:45	0:50
Steps per Training Session	1094	1215	1350	1500
Week Miles from Stepmill	0.62	0.69	0.77	0.85
Weekly Strength Training Miles	2.000	2.000	2.000	2.000
Week Miles Deficit	10.65	11.71	12.87	14.15
Warm-up & Cool-down miles ea. per session	1.33	1.46	1.61	1.77
Backpack Weight	10	11	12	13

Remember that this is for 4 Cardio Training Sessions per Week and walking/jogging/running for Strength Training Warm-Up and Cool-Down.

3x per Week - Mileage Deduction for Strength Training

Weeks 5-8

Training Week	5	6	7	8
Target Vertical	1,255	1,395	1,550	1,722
Target Miles	5.26	5.78	6.36	7.00
Steps	1883	2092	2325	2583
Weekly Hours at 30 SPM	1:02	1:09	1:17	1:26
Minutes each for 3 training sessions	0:20	0:23	0:25	0:28
Steps per Training Session	628	698	775	861
Week Miles from Stepmill	0.27	0.53	0.59	0.65
Weekly Strength Training Miles	2.000	2.000	2.000	2.000
Week Miles Deficit	2.99	3.25	3.77	4.35
Warm-up & Cool-down miles ea. per session	0.50	0.54	0.63	0.72
Backpack Weight	2	3	4	5

Weeks 9-12

Training Week	9	10	11	12
Target Vertical	1,913	2,126	2,362	2,624
Target Miles	7.70	8.47	9.31	10.25
Steps	2870	3189	3543	3937
Weekly Hours at 30 SPM	1:35	1:46	1:58	2:11
Minutes each for 3 training sessions	0:31	0:35	0:39	0:43
Steps per Training Session	957	1063	1181	1313
Week Miles from Stepmill	0.72	0.81	0.89	0.99
Weekly Strength Training Miles	2.000	2.000	2.000	2.000
Week Miles Deficit	4.97	5.66	6.42	7.25
Warm-up & Cool-down miles ea. per session	0.83	0.94	1.07	1.21
Backpack Weight	6	7	8	9

Weeks 13-16

Training Week	13	14	15	16
Target Vertical	2,916	3,240	3,600	4,000
Target Miles	11.27	12.40	13.64	15.00
Steps	4374	4860	5400	6000
Weekly Hours at 30 SPM	2:25	2:42	3:00	3:20
Minutes each for 3 training sessions	0:48	0:54	1:00	1:06
Steps per Training Session	1458	1620	1800	2000
Week Miles from Stepmill	1.10	1.23	1.36	1.52
Weekly Strength Training Miles	2.000	2.000	2.000	2.000
Week Miles Deficit	8.17	9.17	10.27	11.48
Warm-up & Cool-down miles ea. per session	1.36	1.53	1.71	1.91
Backpack Weight	10	11	12	13

Remember that this is for 3 Cardio Training Sessions per Week and walking/jogging/running for Strength Training Warm-Up and Cool-Down.

Summit Success

Stairs Training for Remaining Twelve Weeks

The Stepmill training sessions are in the charts in the section previous. I mention this primarily because if you have an 8" step, you could possibly just go off the Stepmill training charts. I've measured what steps I could find in a few different locations. I've come up with numbers generally between 7" and 9" so you'll need to measure your steps and see where you come in at.

The Stepmill has an 8" rise and a 9" deck. I'm going to assume that if you step up with your heels hanging over the edge a little bit you'll be moving forward about 9" with each step. I kept that consistent between the various charts for Stepmills and Stairs. If you are pretty sure you're moving forward a fair distance you could reduce the amount of warm-up and cool-down for that day.

Now it might not seem that important to you, but the difference between 7" and 9" is between 22% and 28% (depending on the numbers that you're interested in) and that's a LOT of vertical when you're talking about doing 6000 steps in a week.

With that in mind I'm providing a 7" chart group, a 9" chart group, and if your stairs are 8" you can use the Stepmill charts.

Note that the Warm-up and Cool-down Miles column shows the amount of flat walking or running that you would have to do both before and after the Stairs workout for that day.

7" - 4x per Week - no Mileage Deduction for Strength Training

Weeks 5-8

Training Week	5	6	7	8
Target Vertical	1,255	1,395	1,550	1,722
Target Miles	5.26	5.78	6.36	7.00
Steps	2152	2391	2657	2952
Weekly Hours at 30 SPM	1:11	1:19	1:28	1:38
Minutes for 4 training sessions	0:17	0:19	0:22	0:24
Steps per Training Session	538	598	665	738
Week Miles from Stairs	0.31	0.34	0.38	0.42
Week Miles Deficit	4.95	5.44	5.98	6.58
Warm-up & Cool-down miles ea. per session	0.62	0.68	0.75	0.82
Backpack Weight	2	3	4	5

Weeks 9-12

Training Week	9	10	11	12
Target Vertical	1,913	2,126	2,362	2,624
Target Miles	7.70	8.47	9.31	10.25
Steps	3280	3644	4049	4499
Weekly Hours at 30 SPM	1:49	2:01	2:14	2:29
Minutes for 4 training sessions	0:27	0:30	0:33	0:37
Steps per Training Session	820	912	1013	1125
Week Miles from Stairs	0.47	0.52	0.58	0.64
Week Miles Deficit	7.23	7.95	8.74	9.61
Warm-up & Cool-down miles ea. per session	0.90	0.99	1.09	1.20
Backpack Weight	6	7	8	9

Weeks 13-16

Training Week	13	14	15	16
Target Vertical	2,916	3,240	3,600	4,000
Target Miles	11.27	12.40	13.64	15.00
Steps	4999	5554	6171	6857
Weekly Hours at 30 SPM	2:46	3:05	3:25	3:48
Minutes for 4 training sessions	0:41	0:46	0:51	0:57
Steps per Training Session	1250	1389	1543	1715
Week Miles from Stairs	0.71	0.79	0.88	0.97
Week Miles Deficit	10.56	11.61	12.76	14.03
Warm-up & Cool-down miles ea. per session	1.32	1.45	1.59	1.75
Backpack Weight	10	11	12	13

Remember that this is for 4 Cardio Training Sessions per Week with Cross-Training for Strength Training Warm-Up and Cool-Down.

7" - 3x per Week - no Mileage Deduction for Strength Training

Weeks 5-8

Training Week	5	6	7	8
Target Vertical	1,255	1,395	1,550	1,722
Target Miles	5.26	5.78	6.36	7.00
Steps	2152	2391	2657	2952
Weekly Hours at 30 SPM	1:11	1:19	1:28	1:38
Minutes for 4 training sessions	0:17	0:19	0:22	0:24
Steps per Training Session	538	598	665	738
Week Miles from Stairs	0.31	0.34	0.38	0.42
Week Miles Deficit	4.95	5.44	5.98	6.58
Warm-up & Cool-down miles ea. per session	0.62	0.68	0.75	0.82
Backpack Weight	2	3	4	5

Weeks 9-12

Training Week	9	10	11	12
Target Vertical	1,913	2,126	2,362	2,624
Target Miles	7.70	8.47	9.31	10.25
Steps	3280	3644	4049	4499
Weekly Hours at 30 SPM	1:49	2:01	2:14	2:29
Minutes for 4 training sessions	0:27	0:30	0:33	0:37
Steps per Training Session	820	912	1013	1125
Week Miles from Stairs	0.47	0.52	0.58	0.64
Week Miles Deficit	7.23	7.95	8.74	9.61
Warm-up & Cool-down miles ea. per session	0.90	0.99	1.09	1.20
Backpack Weight	6	7	8	9

Weeks 13-16

Training Week	13	14	15	16
Target Vertical	2,916	3,240	3,600	4,000
Target Miles	11.27	12.40	13.64	15.00
Steps	4999	5554	6171	6857
Weekly Hours at 30 SPM	2:46	3:05	3:25	3:48
Minutes for 4 training sessions	0:41	0:46	0:51	0:57
Steps per Training Session	1250	1389	1543	1715
Week Miles from Stairs	0.71	0.79	0.88	0.97
Week Miles Deficit	10.56	11.61	12.76	14.03
Warm-up & Cool-down miles ea. per session	1.32	1.45	1.59	1.75
Backpack Weight	10	11	12	13

Remember that this is for 3 Cardio Training Sessions per Week with Cross-Training for Strength Training Warm-Up and Cool-Down.

7" - 4x per Week - Mileage Deduction for Strength Training

Weeks 5-8

Training Week	5	6	7	8
Target Vertical	1,255	1,395	1,550	1,722
Target Miles	5.26	5.78	6.36	7.00
Steps	2152	2391	2657	2952
Weekly Hours at 30 SPM	1:11	1:19	1:28	1:38
Minutes for 4 training sessions	0:17	0:19	0:22	0:24
Steps per Training Session	538	598	665	738
Week Miles from Stairs	0.31	0.34	0.38	0.42
Weekly Strength Training Miles	2.000	2.000	2.000	2.000
Week Miles Deficit	2.95	3.44	3.98	4.58
Warm-up & Cool-down miles ea. per session	0.37	0.43	0.50	0.57
Backpack Weight	2	3	4	5

Weeks 9-12

Training Week	9	10	11	12
Target Vertical	1,913	2,126	2,362	2,624
Target Miles	7.70	8.47	9.31	10.25
Steps	3280	3644	4049	4499
Weekly Hours at 30 SPM	1:49	2:01	2:14	2:29
Minutes for 4 training sessions	0:27	0:30	0:33	0:37
Steps per Training Session	820	912	1013	1125
Week Miles from Stairs	0.47	0.52	0.58	0.64
Weekly Strength Training Miles	2.000	2.000	2.000	2.000
Week Miles Deficit	5.23	5.95	6.74	7.61
Warm-up & Cool-down miles ea. per session	0.65	0.74	0.84	0.95
Backpack Weight	6	7	8	9

Weeks 13-16

Training Week	13	14	15	16
Target Vertical	2,916	3,240	3,600	4,000
Target Miles	11.27	12.40	13.64	15.00
Steps	4999	5554	6171	6857
Weekly Hours at 30 SPM	2:46	3:05	3:25	3:48
Minutes for 4 training sessions	0:41	0:46	0:51	0:57
Steps per Training Session	1250	1389	1543	1715
Week Miles from Stairs	0.71	0.79	0.88	0.97
Weekly Strength Training Miles	2.000	2.000	2.000	2.000
Week Miles Deficit	8.56	9.61	10.76	12.03
Warm-up & Cool-down miles ea. per session	1.07	1.20	1.34	1.50
Backpack Weight	10	11	12	13

Remember that this is for 4 Cardio Training Sessions per Week and walking/jogging/running for Strength Training Warm-Up and Cool-Down.

7" - 3x per Week - Mileage Deduction for Strength Training

Weeks 5-8

Training Week	5	6	7	8
Target Vertical	1,255	1,395	1,550	1,722
Target Miles	5.26	5.78	6.36	7.00
Steps	2152	2391	2657	2952
Weekly Hours at 30 SPM	1:11	1:19	1:28	1:38
Minutes for 4 training sessions	0:17	0:19	0:22	0:24
Steps per Training Session	538	598	665	738
Week Miles from Stairs	0.31	0.34	0.38	0.42
Weekly Strength Training Miles	2.000	2.000	2.000	2.000
Week Miles Deficit	2.95	3.44	3.98	4.58
Warm-up & Cool-down miles ea. per session	0.37	0.43	0.50	0.57
Backpack Weight	2	3	4	5

Weeks 9-12

Training Week	9	10	11	12
Target Vertical	1,913	2,126	2,362	2,624
Target Miles	7.70	8.47	9.31	10.25
Steps	3280	3644	4049	4499
Weekly Hours at 30 SPM	1:49	2:01	2:14	2:29
Minutes for 4 training sessions	0:27	0:30	0:33	0:37
Steps per Training Session	820	912	1013	1125
Week Miles from Stairs	0.47	0.52	0.58	0.64
Weekly Strength Training Miles	2.000	2.000	2.000	2.000
Week Miles Deficit	5.23	5.95	6.74	7.61
Warm-up & Cool-down miles ea. per session	0.65	0.74	0.84	0.95
Backpack Weight	6	7	8	9

Weeks 13-16

Training Week	13	14	15	16
Target Vertical	2,916	3,240	3,600	4,000
Target Miles	11.27	12.40	13.64	15.00
Steps	4999	5554	6171	6857
Weekly Hours at 30 SPM	2:46	3:05	3:25	3:48
Minutes for 4 training sessions	0:41	0:46	0:51	0:57
Steps per Training Session	1250	1389	1543	1715
Week Miles from Stairs	0.71	0.79	0.88	0.97
Weekly Strength Training Miles	2.000	2.000	2.000	2.000
Week Miles Deficit	8.56	9.61	10.76	12.03
Warm-up & Cool-down miles ea. per session	1.07	1.20	1.34	1.50
Backpack Weight	10	11	12	13

Remember that this is for 3 Cardio Training Sessions per Week and walking/jogging/running for Strength Training Warm-Up and Cool-Down.

9" - 4x per Week - no Mileage Deduction for Strength Training

Weeks 5-8

Training Week	5	6	7	8
Target Vertical	1,255	1,395	1,550	1,722
Target Miles	5.26	5.78	6.36	7.00
Steps	1674	1860	2066	2296
Weekly Hours at 30 SPM	0:55	1:01	1:08	1:16
Minutes for 4 training sessions	0:13	0:15	0:17	0:19
Steps per Training Session	419	465	517	574
Week Miles from Stairs	0.24	0.26	0.29	0.33
Week Miles Deficit	5.02	5.52	6.07	6.67
Warm-up & Cool-down miles ea. per session	0.63	0.69	0.76	0.83
Backpack Weight	2	3	4	5

Weeks 9-12

Training Week	9	10	11	12
Target Vertical	1,913	2,126	2,362	2,624
Target Miles	7.70	8.47	9.31	10.25
Steps	2551	2834	3149	3499
Weekly Hours at 30 SPM	1:25	1:34	1:44	1:56
Minutes for 4 training sessions	0:21	0:23	0:26	0:29
Steps per Training Session	638	709	788	875
Week Miles from Stairs	0.36	0.40	0.45	0.50
Week Miles Deficit	7.34	8.06	8.87	9.75
Warm-up & Cool-down miles ea. per session	0.92	1.01	1.11	1.22
Backpack Weight	6	7	8	9

Weeks 13-16

Training Week	13	14	15	16
Target Vertical	2,916	3,240	3,600	4,000
Target Miles	11.27	12.40	13.64	15.00
Steps	3888	4320	4800	5333
Weekly Hours at 30 SPM	2:09	2:24	2:40	2:57
Minutes for 4 training sessions	0:32	0:36	0:40	0:44
Steps per Training Session	972	1080	1200	1334
Week Miles from Stairs	0.55	0.61	0.68	0.76
Week Miles Deficit	10.72	11.78	12.95	14.24
Warm-up & Cool-down miles ea. per session	1.34	1.47	1.62	1.78
Backpack Weight	10	11	12	13

Remember that this is for 4 Cardio Training Sessions per Week with Cross-Training for Strength Training Warm-Up and Cool-Down.

9" - 3x per Week - no Mileage Deduction for Strength Training

Weeks 5-8

Training Week	5	6	7	8
Target Vertical	1,255	1,395	1,550	1,722
Target Miles	5.26	5.78	6.36	7.00
Steps	1674	1860	2066	2296
Weekly Hours at 30 SPM	0:55	1:01	1:08	1:16
Minutes for 4 training sessions	0:13	0:15	0:17	0:19
Steps per Training Session	419	465	517	574
Week Miles from Stairs	0.24	0.26	0.29	0.33
Week Miles Deficit	5.02	5.52	6.07	6.67
Warm-up & Cool-down miles ea. per session	0.63	0.69	0.76	0.83
Backpack Weight	2	3	4	5

Weeks 9-12

Training Week	9	10	11	12
Target Vertical	1,913	2,126	2,362	2,624
Target Miles	7.70	8.47	9.31	10.25
Steps	2551	2834	3149	3499
Weekly Hours at 30 SPM	1:25	1:34	1:44	1:56
Minutes for 4 training sessions	0:21	0:23	0:26	0:29
Steps per Training Session	638	709	788	875
Week Miles from Stairs	0.36	0.40	0.45	0.50
Week Miles Deficit	7.34	8.06	8.87	9.75
Warm-up & Cool-down miles ea. per session	0.92	1.01	1.11	1.22
Backpack Weight	6	7	8	9

Weeks 13-16

Training Week	13	14	15	16
Target Vertical	2,916	3,240	3,600	4,000
Target Miles	11.27	12.40	13.64	15.00
Steps	3888	4320	4800	5333
Weekly Hours at 30 SPM	2:09	2:24	2:40	2:57
Minutes for 4 training sessions	0:32	0:36	0:40	0:44
Steps per Training Session	972	1080	1200	1334
Week Miles from Stairs	0.55	0.61	0.68	0.76
Week Miles Deficit	10.72	11.78	12.95	14.24
Warm-up & Cool-down miles ea. per session	1.34	1.47	1.62	1.78
Backpack Weight	10	11	12	13

Remember that this is for 3 Cardio Training Sessions per Week with Cross-Training for Strength Training Warm-Up and Cool-Down.

9" - 4x per Week - Mileage Deduction for Strength Training

Weeks 5-8

Training Week	5	6	7	8
Target Vertical	1,255	1,395	1,550	1,722
Target Miles	5.26	5.78	6.36	7.00
Steps	1674	1860	2066	2296
Weekly Hours at 30 SPM	0:55	1:01	1:08	1:16
Minutes for 4 training sessions	0:13	0:15	0:17	0:19
Steps per Training Session	419	465	517	574
Week Miles from Stairs	0.24	0.26	0.29	0.33
Weekly Strength Training Miles	2.000	2.000	2.000	2.000
Week Miles Deficit	3.02	3.52	4.07	4.67
Warm-up & Cool-down miles ea. per session	0.38	0.44	0.51	0.58
Backpack Weight	2	3	4	5

Weeks 9-12

Training Week	9	10	11	12
Target Vertical	1,913	2,126	2,362	2,624
Target Miles	7.70	8.47	9.31	10.25
Steps	2551	2834	3149	3499
Weekly Hours at 30 SPM	1:25	1:34	1:44	1:56
Minutes for 4 training sessions	0:21	0:23	0:26	0:29
Steps per Training Session	638	709	788	875
Week Miles from Stairs	0.36	0.40	0.45	0.50
Weekly Strength Training Miles	2.000	2.000	2.000	2.000
Week Miles Deficit	5.34	6.06	6.87	7.75
Warm-up & Cool-down miles ea. per session	0.67	0.76	0.86	0.97
Backpack Weight	6	7	8	9

Weeks 13-16

Training Week	13	14	15	16
Target Vertical	2,916	3,240	3,600	4,000
Target Miles	11.27	12.40	13.64	15.00
Steps	3888	4320	4800	5333
Weekly Hours at 30 SPM	2:09	2:24	2:40	2:57
Minutes for 4 training sessions	0:32	0:36	0:40	0:44
Steps per Training Session	972	1080	1200	1334
Week Miles from Stairs	0.55	0.61	0.68	0.76
Weekly Strength Training Miles	2.000	2.000	2.000	2.000
Week Miles Deficit	8.72	9.78	10.95	12.24
Warm-up & Cool-down miles ea. per session	1.09	1.22	1.37	1.53
Backpack Weight	10	11	12	13

Remember that this is for 4 Cardio Training Sessions per Week and walking/jogging/running for Strength Training Warm-Up and Cool-Down.

9" - 3x per Week - Mileage Deduction for Strength Training

Weeks 5-8

Training Week	5	6	7	8
Target Vertical	1,255	1,395	1,550	1,722
Target Miles	5.26	5.78	6.36	7.00
Steps	1674	1860	2066	2296
Weekly Hours at 30 SPM	0:55	1:01	1:08	1:16
Minutes each for 3 training sessions	0:13	0:15	0:17	0:19
Steps per Training Session	419	465	517	574
Week Miles from Stairs	0.24	0.26	0.29	0.33
Weekly Strength Training Miles	2.000	2.000	2.000	2.000
Week Miles Deficit	3.02	3.52	4.07	4.67
Warm-up & Cool-down miles ea. per session	0.38	0.44	0.51	0.58
Backpack Weight	2	3	4	5

Weeks 9-12

Training Week	9	10	11	12
Target Vertical	1,913	2,126	2,362	2,624
Target Miles	7.70	8.47	9.31	10.25
Steps	2551	2834	3149	3499
Weekly Hours at 30 SPM	1:25	1:34	1:44	1:56
Minutes each for 3 training sessions	0:21	0:23	0:26	0:29
Steps per Training Session	638	709	788	875
Week Miles from Stairs	0.36	0.40	0.45	0.50
Weekly Strength Training Miles	2.000	2.000	2.000	2.000
Week Miles Deficit	5.34	6.06	6.87	7.75
Warm-up & Cool-down miles ea. per session	0.67	0.76	0.86	0.97
Backpack Weight	6	7	8	9

Weeks 13-16

Training Week	13	14	15	16
Target Vertical	2,916	3,240	3,600	4,000
Target Miles	11.27	12.40	13.64	15.00
Steps	3888	4320	4800	5333
Weekly Hours at 30 SPM	2:09	2:24	2:40	2:57
Minutes each for 3 training sessions	0:32	0:36	0:40	0:44
Steps per Training Session	972	1080	1200	1334
Week Miles from Stairs	0.55	0.61	0.68	0.76
Weekly Strength Training Miles	2.000	2.000	2.000	2.000
Week Miles Deficit	8.72	9.78	10.95	12.24
Warm-up & Cool-down miles ea. per session	1.09	1.22	1.37	1.53
Backpack Weight	10	11	12	13

Remember that this is for 3 Cardio Training Sessions per Week and walking/jogging/running for Strength Training Warm-Up and Cool-Down.

Box Stepping Training for Remaining 12 Weeks

You're going to finish this out on a 12" box now. That's about as high as most normal people should go and try to maintain endurance at 30 steps per minute. I'm going to go ahead and include 15" in the charts, in case we have some really strong and fast people doing this program. If you're one of them I'd love to hear from you.

I'm going to allow for a horizontal distance each training day, though I'm showing variations for stepping sideways, over and back, back, and forward box stepping. I'm not convinced that there actually is a measurable horizontal movement, but when I plug in the numbers it's so tiny that it's not worth bickering over. I'll leave it in. But keep in mind that you're going to have to make up a huge mileage deficit each week to make up for the quick vertical gain.

12" - 4x per Week - no Mileage Deduction for Strength Training

Weeks 5-8

Training Week	5	6	7	8
Target Vertical	1,255	1,395	1,550	1,722
Target Miles	5.26	5.78	6.36	7.00
Steps	1255	1395	1550	1722
Weekly Hours at 30 SPM	0:41	0:46	0:51	0:57
Minutes for 4 training sessions	0:10	0:11	0:12	0:14
Steps per Training Session	314	349	388	431
Week Miles from Box	0.18	0.20	0.22	0.24
Week Miles Deficit	5.08	5.59	6.14	6.75
Warm-up & Cool-down miles ea. per session	0.63	0.70	0.77	0.84
Backpack Weight	2	3	4	5

Weeks 9-12

Training Week	9	10	11	12
Target Vertical	1,913	2,126	2,362	2,624
Target Miles	7.70	8.47	9.31	10.25
Steps	1913	2126	2362	2624
Weekly Hours at 30 SPM	1:03	1:10	1:18	1:27
Minutes for 4 training sessions	0:15	0:17	0:19	0:21
Steps per Training Session	479	532	591	657
Week Miles from Box	0.27	0.30	0.34	0.37
Week Miles Deficit	7.43	8.17	8.98	9.87
Warm-up & Cool-down miles ea. per session	0.93	1.02	1.12	1.23
Backpack Weight	6	7	8	9

Weeks 13-16

Training Week	13	14	15	16
Target Vertical	2,916	3,240	3,600	4,000
Target Miles	11.27	12.40	13.64	15.00
Steps	2916	3240	3600	4000
Weekly Hours at 30 SPM	1:37	1:48	2:00	2:13
Minutes for 4 training sessions	0:24	0:27	0:30	0:33
Steps per Training Session	729	810	900	1000
Week Miles from Box	0.41	0.46	0.51	0.57
Week Miles Deficit	10.86	11.94	13.13	14.43
Warm-up & Cool-down miles ea. per session	1.36	1.49	1.64	1.80
Backpack Weight	10	11	12	13

Remember that this is for 4 Cardio Training Sessions per Week with Cross-Training for Strength Training Warm-Up and Cool-Down.

12" - 3x per Week - no Mileage Deduction for Strength Training

Weeks 5-8

Training Week	5	6	7	8
Target Vertical	1,255	1,395	1,550	1,722
Target Miles	5.26	5.78	6.36	7.00
Steps	1255	1395	1550	1722
Weekly Hours at 30 SPM	0:41	0:46	0:51	0:57
Minutes for 3 training sessions	0:10	0:11	0:12	0:14
Steps per Training Session	314	349	388	431
Week Miles from Box	0.18	0.20	0.22	0.24
Week Miles Deficit	5.08	5.59	6.14	6.75
Warm-up & Cool-down miles ea. per session	0.63	0.70	0.77	0.84
Backpack Weight	2	3	4	5

Weeks 9-12

Training Week	9	10	11	12
Target Vertical	1,913	2,126	2,362	2,624
Target Miles	7.70	8.47	9.31	10.25
Steps	1913	2126	2362	2624
Weekly Hours at 30 SPM	1:03	1:10	1:18	1:27
Minutes for 3 training sessions	0:15	0:17	0:19	0:21
Steps per Training Session	479	532	591	657
Week Miles from Box	0.27	0.30	0.34	0.37
Week Miles Deficit	7.43	8.17	8.98	9.87
Warm-up & Cool-down miles ea. per session	0.93	1.02	1.12	1.23
Backpack Weight	6	7	8	9

Weeks 13-16

Training Week	13	14	15	16
Target Vertical	2,916	3,240	3,600	4,000
Target Miles	11.27	12.40	13.64	15.00
Steps	2916	3240	3600	4000
Weekly Hours at 30 SPM	1:37	1:48	2:00	2:13
Minutes for 3 training sessions	0:24	0:27	0:30	0:33
Steps per Training Session	729	810	900	1000
Week Miles from Box	0.41	0.46	0.51	0.57
Week Miles Deficit	10.86	11.94	13.13	14.43
Warm-up & Cool-down miles ea. per session	1.36	1.49	1.64	1.80
Backpack Weight	10	11	12	13

Remember that this is for 3 Cardio Training Sessions per Week with Cross-Training for Strength Training Warm-Up and Cool-Down.

12" - 4x per Week - Mileage Deduction for Strength Training

Weeks 5-8

Training Week	5	6	7	8
Target Vertical	1,255	1,395	1,550	1,722
Target Miles	5.26	5.78	6.36	7.00
Steps	1255	1395	1550	1722
Weekly Hours at 30 SPM	0:41	0:46	0:51	0:57
Minutes for 4 training sessions	0:10	0:11	0:12	0:14
Steps per Training Session	314	349	388	431
Week Miles from Box	0.18	0.20	0.22	0.24
Weekly Strength Training Miles	2.000	2.000	2.000	2.000
Week Miles Deficit	3.08	3.59	4.14	4.75
Warm-up & Cool-down miles ea. per session	0.38	0.45	0.52	0.59
Backpack Weight	2	3	4	5

Weeks 9-12

Training Week	9	10	11	12
Target Vertical	1,913	2,126	2,362	2,624
Target Miles	7.70	8.47	9.31	10.25
Steps	1913	2126	2362	2624
Weekly Hours at 30 SPM	1:03	1:10	1:18	1:27
Minutes for 4 training sessions	0:15	0:17	0:19	0:21
Steps per Training Session	479	532	591	657
Week Miles from Box	0.27	0.30	0.34	0.37
Weekly Strength Training Miles	2.000	2.000	2.000	2.000
Week Miles Deficit	5.43	6.17	6.98	7.87
Warm-up & Cool-down miles ea. per session	0.68	0.77	0.87	0.98
Backpack Weight	6	7	8	9

Weeks 13-16

Training Week	13	14	15	16
Target Vertical	2,916	3,240	3,600	4,000
Target Miles	11.27	12.40	13.64	15.00
Steps	2916	3240	3600	4000
Weekly Hours at 30 SPM	1:37	1:48	2:00	2:13
Minutes for 4 training sessions	0:24	0:27	0:30	0:33
Steps per Training Session	729	810	900	1000
Week Miles from Box	0.41	0.46	0.51	0.57
Weekly Strength Training Miles	2.000	2.000	2.000	2.000
Week Miles Deficit	8.86	9.94	11.13	12.43
Warm-up & Cool-down miles ea. per session	1.11	1.24	1.39	1.55
Backpack Weight	10	11	12	13

Remember that this is for 4 Cardio Training Sessions per Week and walking/jogging/running for Strength Training Warm-Up and Cool-Down.

12" - 3x per Week - Mileage Deduction for Strength Training

Weeks 5-8

Training Week	5	6	7	8
Target Vertical	1,255	1,395	1,550	1,722
Target Miles	5.26	5.78	6.36	7.00
Steps	1255	1395	1550	1722
Weekly Hours at 30 SPM	0:41	0:46	0:51	0:57
Minutes for 3 training sessions	0:10	0:11	0:12	0:14
Steps per Training Session	314	349	388	431
Week Miles from Box	0.18	0.20	0.22	0.24
Weekly Strength Training Miles	2.000	2.000	2.000	2.000
Week Miles Deficit	3.08	3.59	4.14	4.75
Warm-up & Cool-down miles ea. per session	0.38	0.45	0.52	0.59
Backpack Weight	2	3	4	5

Weeks 9-12

Training Week	9	10	11	12
Target Vertical	1,913	2,126	2,362	2,624
Target Miles	7.70	8.47	9.31	10.25
Steps	1913	2126	2362	2624
Weekly Hours at 30 SPM	1:03	1:10	1:18	1:27
Minutes for 3 training sessions	0:15	0:17	0:19	0:21
Steps per Training Session	479	532	591	657
Week Miles from Box	0.27	0.30	0.34	0.37
Weekly Strength Training Miles	2.000	2.000	2.000	2.000
Week Miles Deficit	5.43	6.17	6.98	7.87
Warm-up & Cool-down miles ea. per session	0.68	0.77	0.87	0.98
Backpack Weight	6	7	8	9

Weeks 13-16

Training Week	13	14	15	16
Target Vertical	2,916	3,240	3,600	4,000
Target Miles	11.27	12.40	13.64	15.00
Steps	2916	3240	3600	4000
Weekly Hours at 30 SPM	1:37	1:48	2:00	2:13
Minutes for 3 training sessions	0:24	0:27	0:30	0:33
Steps per Training Session	729	810	900	1000
Week Miles from Box	0.41	0.46	0.51	0.57
Weekly Strength Training Miles	2.000	2.000	2.000	2.000
Week Miles Deficit	8.86	9.94	11.13	12.43
Warm-up & Cool-down miles ea. per session	1.11	1.24	1.39	1.55
Backpack Weight	10	11	12	13

Remember that this is for 3 Cardio Training Sessions per Week and walking/jogging/running for Strength Training Warm-Up and Cool-Down.

15" - 4x per Week - no Mileage Deduction for Strength Training

Weeks 5-8

Training Week	5	6	7	8
Target Vertical	1,255	1,395	1,550	1,722
Target Miles	5.26	5.78	6.36	7.00
Steps	1004	1116	1240	1377
Weekly Hours at 30 SPM	0:33	0:37	0:41	0:45
Minutes for 4 training sessions	0:08	0:09	0:10	0:11
Steps per Training Session	252	279	310	345
Week Miles from Box	0.14	0.16	0.18	0.20
Week Miles Deficit	5.11	5.62	6.19	6.80
Warm-up & Cool-down miles ea. per session	0.64	0.70	0.77	0.85
Backpack Weight	2	3	4	5

Weeks 9-12

Training Week	9	10	11	12
Target Vertical	1,913	2,126	2,362	2,624
Target Miles	7.70	8.47	9.31	10.25
Steps	1531	1701	1890	2100
Weekly Hours at 30 SPM	0:51	0:56	1:02	1:09
Minutes for 4 training sessions	0:12	0:14	0:15	0:17
Steps per Training Session	383	426	473	525
Week Miles from Box	0.22	0.24	0.27	0.30
Week Miles Deficit	7.48	8.23	9.05	9.95
Warm-up & Cool-down miles ea. per session	0.93	1.03	1.13	1.24
Backpack Weight	6	7	8	9

Weeks 13-16

Training Week	13	14	15	16
Target Vertical	2,916	3,240	3,600	4,000
Target Miles	11.27	12.40	13.64	15.00
Steps	2333	2592	2880	3200
Weekly Hours at 30 SPM	1:17	1:26	1:36	1:46
Minutes for 4 training sessions	0:19	0:21	0:24	0:26
Steps per Training Session	584	648	720	800
Week Miles from Box	0.33	0.37	0.41	0.45
Week Miles Deficit	10.94	12.03	13.23	14.55
Warm-up & Cool-down miles ea. per session	1.37	1.50	1.65	1.82
Backpack Weight	10	11	12	13

Remember that this is for 4 Cardio Training Sessions per Week with Cross-Training for Strength Training Warm-Up and Cool-Down.

15" - 3x per Week - no Mileage Deduction for Strength Training

Weeks 5-8

Training Week	5	6	7	8
Target Vertical	1,255	1,395	1,550	1,722
Target Miles	5.26	5.78	6.36	7.00
Steps	1004	1116	1240	1377
Weekly Hours at 30 SPM	0:33	0:37	0:41	0:45
Minutes for 3 training sessions	0:08	0:09	0:10	0:11
Steps per Training Session	252	279	310	345
Week Miles from Box	0.14	0.16	0.18	0.20
Week Miles Deficit	5.11	5.62	6.19	6.80
Warm-up & Cool-down miles ea. per session	0.64	0.70	0.77	0.85
Backpack Weight	2	3	4	5

Weeks 9-12

Training Week	9	10	11	12
Target Vertical	1,913	2,126	2,362	2,624
Target Miles	7.70	8.47	9.31	10.25
Steps	1531	1701	1890	2100
Weekly Hours at 30 SPM	0:51	0:56	1:02	1:09
Minutes for 3 training sessions	0:12	0:14	0:15	0:17
Steps per Training Session	383	426	473	525
Week Miles from Box	0.22	0.24	0.27	0.30
Week Miles Deficit	7.48	8.23	9.05	9.95
Warm-up & Cool-down miles ea. per session	0.93	1.03	1.13	1.24
Backpack Weight	6	7	8	9

Weeks 13-16

Training Week	13	14	15	16
Target Vertical	2,916	3,240	3,600	4,000
Target Miles	11.27	12.40	13.64	15.00
Steps	2333	2592	2880	3200
Weekly Hours at 30 SPM	1:17	1:26	1:36	1:46
Minutes for 3 training sessions	0:19	0:21	0:24	0:26
Steps per Training Session	584	648	720	800
Week Miles from Box	0.33	0.37	0.41	0.45
Week Miles Deficit	10.94	12.03	13.23	14.55
Warm-up & Cool-down miles ea. per session	1.37	1.50	1.65	1.82
Backpack Weight	10	11	12	13

Remember that this is for 3 Cardio Training Sessions per Week with Cross-Training for Strength Training Warm-Up and Cool-Down.

15" - 4x per Week - Mileage Deduction for Strength Training

Weeks 5-8

Training Week	5	6	7	8
Target Vertical	1,255	1,395	1,550	1,722
Target Miles	5.26	5.78	6.36	7.00
Steps	1004	1116	1240	1377
Weekly Hours at 30 SPM	0:33	0:37	0:41	0:45
Minutes for 4 training sessions	0:08	0:09	0:10	0:11
Steps per Training Session	252	279	310	345
Week Miles from Box	0.14	0.16	0.18	0.20
Weekly Strength Training Miles	2.000	2.000	2.000	2.000
Week Miles Deficit	3.11	3.62	4.19	4.80
Warm-up & Cool-down miles ea. per session	0.39	0.45	0.52	0.60
Backpack Weight	2	3	4	5

Weeks 9-12

Training Week	9	10	11	12
Target Vertical	1,913	2,126	2,362	2,624
Target Miles	7.70	8.47	9.31	10.25
Steps	1531	1701	1890	2100
Weekly Hours at 30 SPM	0:51	0:56	1:02	1:09
Minutes for 4 training sessions	0:12	0:14	0:15	0:17
Steps per Training Session	383	426	473	525
Week Miles from Box	0.22	0.24	0.27	0.30
Weekly Strength Training Miles	2.000	2.000	2.000	2.000
Week Miles Deficit	5.48	6.23	7.05	7.95
Warm-up & Cool-down miles ea. per session	0.68	0.78	0.88	0.99
Backpack Weight	6	7	8	9

Summit Success

Weeks 13-16

Training Week	13	14	15	16
Target Vertical	2,916	3,240	3,600	4,000
Target Miles	11.27	12.40	13.64	15.00
Steps	2333	2592	2880	3200
Weekly Hours at 30 SPM	1:17	1:26	1:36	1:46
Minutes for 4 training sessions	0:19	0:21	0:24	0:26
Steps per Training Session	584	648	720	800
Week Miles from Box	0.33	0.37	0.41	0.45
Weekly Strength Training Miles	2.000	2.000	2.000	2.000
Week Miles Deficit	8.94	10.03	11.23	12.55
Warm-up & Cool-down miles ea. per session	1.12	1.25	1.40	1.57
Backpack Weight	10	11	12	13

Remember that this is for 4 Cardio Training Sessions per Week and walking/jogging/running for Strength Training Warm-Up and Cool-Down.

15" - 3x per Week - Mileage Deduction for Strength Training

Weeks 5-8

Training Week	5	6	7	8
Target Vertical	1,255	1,395	1,550	1,722
Target Miles	5.26	5.78	6.36	7.00
Steps	1004	1116	1240	1377
Weekly Hours at 30 SPM	0:33	0:37	0:41	0:45
Minutes for 4 training sessions	0:08	0:09	0:10	0:11
Steps per Training Session	252	279	310	345
Week Miles from Box	0.14	0.16	0.18	0.20
Weekly Strength Training Miles	2.000	2.000	2.000	2.000
Week Miles Deficit	3.11	3.62	4.19	4.80
Warm-up & Cool-down miles ea. per session	0.39	0.45	0.52	0.60
Backpack Weight	2	3	4	5

Weeks 9-12

Training Week	9	10	11	12
Target Vertical	1,913	2,126	2,362	2,624
Target Miles	7.70	8.47	9.31	10.25
Steps	1531	1701	1890	2100
Weekly Hours at 30 SPM	0:51	0:56	1:02	1:09
Minutes for 4 training sessions	0:12	0:14	0:15	0:17
Steps per Training Session	383	426	473	525
Week Miles from Box	0.22	0.24	0.27	0.30
Weekly Strength Training Miles	2.000	2.000	2.000	2.000
Week Miles Deficit	5.48	6.23	7.05	7.95
Warm-up & Cool-down miles ea. per session	0.68	0.78	0.88	0.99
Backpack Weight	6	7	8	9

Weeks 13-16

Training Week	13	14	15	16
Target Vertical	2,916	3,240	3,600	4,000
Target Miles	11.27	12.40	13.64	15.00
Steps	2333	2592	2880	3200
Weekly Hours at 30 SPM	1:17	1:26	1:36	1:46
Minutes for 4 training sessions	0:19	0:21	0:24	0:26
Steps per Training Session	584	648	720	800
Week Miles from Box	0.33	0.37	0.41	0.45
Weekly Strength Training Miles	2.000	2.000	2.000	2.000
Week Miles Deficit	8.94	10.03	11.23	12.55
Warm-up & Cool-down miles ea. per session	1.12	1.25	1.40	1.57
Backpack Weight	10	11	12	13

Remember that this is for 3 Cardio Training Sessions per Week and walking/jogging/running for Strength Training Warm-Up and Cool-Down.

Ending the Sixteen Weeks

This program is all about getting ready to do a 14er or big dream hike after 16 weeks. If you're going to hurry up and do that near the end of this program, try to give yourself two weeks to cut back and relax. Go back two or three columns in the chart for a week and then go do your 14er or other goal hike or climb. Don't train for about three days before you hike it so you're fresh and ready to go. This is called tapering and we're not going to do any fancy taper schedules. Just cut back for a couple weeks and then take a few days off.

If it's going to be a while before your big hike then it would probably be best to repeat week 16 for a week, take a week off, then repeat Weeks 9-12 over and over. Notice how I put those into separate charts for all the different exercises? Then when you have about five weeks to go before your big goal hike or climb, go ahead and do Weeks 13-16 and then take a week off. You'll be in awesome shape then. It's a great way to maintain your fitness as you wait it out for the next book. Stay tuned for the exciting news about that one.

If you want to cut back a little bit on your cardio, maybe do Weeks 5-8 over and over, you could spend a bit more time on your weights and strength training and focus on making progress there for a few months. After 12 weeks of that then go ahead on to Weeks 9-12 for about 12 weeks. This is about six months of working into a base level of fitness to prepare you for going on to Weeks 13-16 and peaking for a big hike or climb. It will get you in great shape to be fully prepared for the next training manual. Be prepared.

Mixing it up

It would be fairly easy to do this program just on a treadmill and get in enough vertical and enough miles in a week. If so I highly recommend you mix it up and do:
- one fourth of your vertical at 6%
- one fourth of your vertical at 9%
- one fourth of your vertical at 12%
- one fourth of your vertical at 15%

That way you have a good combination of miles and vertical that also somewhat simulates actual trail conditions.

If you have access to an Incline Treadmill, you can do the same thing in extended cycles, perhaps
- one sixth of your vertical at 6%
- one sixth of your vertical at 12%
- one sixth of your vertical at 16%
- one sixth of your vertical at 24%
- one sixth of your vertical at 32%
- one sixth of your vertical at 40%

With this plan you might have to do an extra few miles at 3% to get in your miles for the week, but it's short work to get in vertical at 32% and 40%. You should have that extra time on hand.

If you want to spend a lot of time on a Stepmill that gets in your vertical pretty easily, but you'll end up a bit short on miles. Actually a lot short on miles. I recommend then that you do about two-thirds to three-fourths of your vertical on the Stairmaster and the rest on the treadmill at 3-6%. The stairs cut you short on miles that much, as I've pointed out several times now in this book. You can also just get in all your vertical on the Stepmill and go for long pleasant walks outside and get in some valuable Me-Time.

You could also do two longer sessions, one on a treadmill and one on a Stairmaster to get in your vertical weekly goal, then your third or fourth cardio training session could be on an elliptical or bicycle and just consider it cross-training. As long as you get in your miles and your vertical, if you have time left over in the week, any good conditioning cardio will be of benefit in the big scheme of things.

If you really want to mix it up, you can get in a lot of vertical quickly with the stairs or box stepping, or the Stepmill and a treadmill or Incline Treadmill set steeply for three really different sessions of training. Then for the fourth session just go for a long walk or run to get in your miles.

I'm not trying to make things more complicated, but providing some options for you to consider so you can see just how free and easy this program really can be. Coming next though, is a selection of training cycle prescriptions based on this information to make it simple to decide what to do. Just select the path that fits where you are in your own ability to train and make it work for you.

Now What?

You wanted to train for a 14er. I'm hoping that by the end of this you've gone and done it. I'm hoping you posted your best training photos on my Facebook Page at http://www.facebook.com/SevenSummitsBody. I'm hoping you've climbed your mountain and posted those photos as well. I hope that you took part in some lively discussions and helped motivate and inspire others to great success in accomplishing this goal.

What's next? You want to climb more? Do two or three 14ers the same day? Do a backpacking trip up to climb a few mountains over a weekend or even a week? Maybe the Seven Summits Quest? Let me know what your goals are and let's see how we can help each other. Remember I have special additional content available at http://sevensummitsbody.com/summitsuccess so go check it out see what more I have in store for you.

What I don't want you to do is decide that you've achieved your goal and you completely stop training and making progress. I want you to springboard off this goal and set another. Try climbing 5 Fourteeners in 5 days. Get some skills and glacier climb Rainier (WA 14er) and rock climb Whitney (CA 14er) on a roped team. Go to Ecuador for some of the most fun and beautiful 5000 meter peaks in the world.

Whatever comes next for you, drop by my author or fitness blogs and leave a comment. Come to my Facebook pages and post photos. We'd all love to see your success in action. Go to the website you bought this from and leave your honest evaluation and review of this book and program. I'd love to keep working with you and every comment I get is a chance for me to improve and become a better trainer and coach. Thanks

About the Author

Charles Miske lives and trains in Summit County Colorado at 9,300'. He regularly climbs 14ers and runs trails year round. He's been climbing the Seven Summits and Volcanic Seven Summits and enjoys world travel and trekking. While not training he manages to squeeze in writing about his adventures in the mountains (Seven Summits Quest Series) and runs a consulting business. If you want to know more, please visit his blog at http://charlesmiske.com and check out his other books.

Coming 2015 – Part Two of this book, with more advanced training.

Made in the USA
San Bernardino, CA
10 December 2016